FASCINATION
OF DECAY

Ruin Room (see page 238)

FASCINATION
OF DECAY

Ruins: Relic–Symbol–Ornament

PAUL ZUCKER

The Gregg Press

RIDGEWOOD, NEW JERSEY

310

Contents

vii

Preface

The influence of individual associations and private experiences upon visual perception goes much further than generally believed. The aim of this book is to explore the roots of the emotional and intellectual effects of ruins, in all their psychological complexity, during different historical epochs. The story of these manifold reactions, as well as the factual information, should represent an indirect contribution to the history of ideas.

So many individuals and institutions here and abroad have helped during the preparation for this book that it would be impossible to acknowledge their kindness in detail, and the omission of some names is certainly not intentional and may be forgiven. Many museums and private collectors were most generous in providing photographs and information; my special thanks go to the Metropolitan Museum of Art, the Cooper Union Museum, The Museum of Modern Art, the Public Library and the Avery Library, New York, and to the Fototeca di Architettura e Topografia dell'Italia Antica, Rome.

Among my colleagues and friends, Mr. Hyatt Mayor, formerly curator of the Print Dept., Metropolitan Museum of Art; Professor Thomas J. McCormick, Vassar College Art Gallery (now in London); Dr. Gerd Muehsam, Donnell Library; the late Professor Carroll L. V. Meeks, Yale University; Dr. Ernest Nash, American Academy, Rome; Donald Oenslager, New York; Dr. Richard P. Wunder, Smithsonian Institute, Washington, D. C. are those to whom I feel mostly indebted for their interest and valuable advice. I feel especially obliged to Mr. Fred C. Sawyer of The Gregg Press, Inc. for his untiring editorial cooperation, and last not least, to Dr. Lotte Pulvermacher-Egers for her understanding assistance and research from the very beginning to the end.

P. Z.

WHY RUINS?

Why Ruins?

A ruin exists in a state of continual transition caused by natural deterioration, specific catastrophes, or other circumstances. But the changing concept of the ruin is based not only on its objective appearance, but is equally dependent on the individuality of the beholder. His reaction will reflect his emotional attitudes, his cultural and intellectual level; but, even more, the prevalent concepts of his time: the "Zeitgeist."

Although the ruin still continues to exist in the sphere of life, life has departed from it, and we are aware only of a more or less well-preserved fragment of an earlier age. And this fragment will be perceived and interpreted in various ways: either out of antiquarian-archeological interest, or as a reflection of the Freudian "death instinct," or from the point of view of melancholy fascination, or as mere fanciful enjoyment of decoration.

The objective of this study is to analyze the aesthetics of ruins and to discover the reason for their fascination. Neither an archeological nor an historical survey of ruins is intended, nor is a complete treatment of the subject the aim. The results of excavations and measurements, or the state of preservation, or even the development of certain stylistic forms are of secondary importance only. The accent is on the relationship, as it is mirrored in all fields of visual art in Western civilization, between Ruin and Man. Therefore, the image of the ruin, as it appears in painting and in the graphic arts, in stage setting and in artificial garden architecture, becomes as much an echo of the variety of feelings in 'the interpreter's cultural climate as that of the age in which the building was constructed. Changing from country to country, from century to century, sometimes from generation to generation, the image of the ruin is always ambivalent and open to manifold interpretations.

Functional values which the ruin might have possessed originally are of even less value in its aesthetic interpretation. If structurally adapted to the needs of later centuries, ruins lose their character as ruins. Details may be interesting, aesthetically or merely from an archeological point of view. They are often depicted clearly enough even in otherwise completely romantic interpretations. Without details, only the most basic values remain: proportions, the interrelationship of space and volume, and, of course, the significance of the ruin to the artist.

2

Just as we cannot imagine the sounds and colors of the music of Vivaldi or Mozart exactly as the composers conceived them, so it is impossible for us to perceive the original proportions and interrelationships of space and volume in a ruin; to see it with the eyes of the architect who planned it. Here is the crux of the aesthetic problem. Only rarely have the proportional and spatial qualities of the original creation survived without concealment, modification, or partial destruction. The past lies as much in the realm of the imagination as does the future.

For this reason, ruins stemming from non-Western civilizations; ruins such as the Egyptian Abu Simbel, the Hindu Kailasa Temple in Elura, the Mayan ruins of Uxmal in Yucatán, or the Khmer Temple in Angkor Wat, Indochina, will not be discussed. The impressions which we receive from them are much more complex than those which we receive from Western monuments. The original structure was usually so remote from our traditional and innate concepts of architecture, that our primary interest in it will always be centered in its exotic character. Therefore, the changes brought about by its present ruinous condition will not produce the same aesthetic response that we get as we stand before a relic of Western civilization.

Devastated by time or by willful destruction, incomplete as they are, ruins represent a combination of created, man-made forms and organic nature. They can no longer be considered genuine works of art, since the original intention of the builder has been more or less lost. Nor can they be taken as an outgrowth of nature, since man-made elements continue to exist as a basis for that which has been contributed or taken away by Time, in its vindictiveness toward human creations.

Although ruins exist in this sphere between Art and Nature; formed by both, molded by the unforeseeable sequence of changes and chances in history, there always remains an aesthetic unity dominated by whatever has been preserved as fragments of the original architecture. In contrast, partially destroyed paintings or mutilated sculpture lose irreplaceably their aesthetic unity, with the exception of the torso, which represents an aesthetic problem of its own.

An attempt to enumerate the various reactions and emotional responses to ruins through the centuries would be merely mechanical and would not lead to a better understanding of the problem—each attempt at segmentation of the flow of history would appear arbitrary. We must turn to poetry, letters, and diaries; to paintings and works of graphic art which can convey to later generations how earlier centuries felt about ruins *in situ*. Whether we perceive a ruin primarily as an expression of an eerie, romantic mood, as a palpable documentation of a period in the past, or as something which recalls a specific concept of architectural space and proportion, the ruin evokes in us a feeling of the impact of history on the living.

Sotalbo

Corner of a Castle. Late Medieval (Fifteenth Century). Photo Courtesy of José Ortiz Echagüe. The Museum of Modern Art, New York

WHY RUINS?

The vindictive character of Nature toward the work of human hands is clearly revealed in these ruins of the castle of Sotalbo (Province of Avila, Spain). Late medieval walls and towers are inextricably fused into primeval masses of chaotic boulders. And yet, even these few fragments of a rude, vernacular architecture in the last stages of decay, partially carved out of live rock above ground, are sufficient to make us conscious of the contrast between Nature and the organizing power of the human spirit. We are fully aware that the same forces which have shaped the outlines of mountains or the banks of a river have also molded the visible contours of the original architecture into a striking image of deformation. Here, as in the better-known ruins of Les Baux in France, a popular tourist attraction whose arches and vaults stem from the same century, a new complex whole—a *Gestalt* has come into being; not an aesthetic unity, but definitely more than a mere heap of stones. Nature has used elements of architecture as objects, just as art takes as object elements of Nature.

Agrigento, Sicily

Temple of Castor and Pollux. Fifth Century B.C. Photo, Italian State Tourist Office, New York

Only four of the original thirty-four Doric peripheral columns are left, yet the unsophisticated beholder does not get the impression of a "ruin" when he looks at these fragments of an ancient temple; in contrast to his reaction to the ruins of Sotalbo. The erosion of the stone, and the few patches of stucco and paint which remain, are hardly perceived as symptoms of decay. One almost forgets that these columns were at one time only parts of a great architectural structure. They affect us rather as abstract sculpture whose three-dimensional qualities are so strong that their forms are enjoyed in themselves. Their classical proportions, their rhythm, and their texture are so expressive that no desire is evoked to reconstruct the whole of the temple in our imagination. Nor do they give vent to any melancholy thoughts about the transience of human life.

THE BEGINNING

The Beginning

Although Boccaccio, writing in the fourteenth century, describes some ruins in the vicinity of Baiai as "old stones and yet new for modern souls," the conscious awareness of ruins as such did not develop until the early Renaissance. Then, the discovery and appreciation of ancient monuments became a preoccupation. We can read medieval books which tell of Biblical catastrophes such as the destruction of Babel, Jericho, or Sodom, or Greek myths which describe the burning of Troy, but we can scarcely visualize those places. In the Renaissance, however, there were palpable, measurable vestiges of classical antiquity, together with re-discovered literary sources to open the eyes of the living for what the dead had left behind. Suddenly people began to notice ruins which for many centuries had been passed by with indifference. Evidence of this new awareness of ruins appears in one of the most outstanding early Italian books—the *Hypnerotomachia Polifili* by Francesco Colonna.

Colonna's older contemporaries, Leone Battista Alberti, the most important fifteenth-century architectural theoretician, and Antonio Francesco di Filarete wrote treatises which were basic for all Italian Renaissance architects. But these men, in contrast to Colonna, were in no way interested in ruins *per se*. Most of their architectural designs served later as guides for the reconstruction of ancient buildings and as textbooks of ornamental design.

This was also true of their successors in the sixteenth century—the standard-bearers of the Italian High Renaissance—whose books became architectural classics for centuries to come. These voluminous atlases, like the anatomical tomes from Leonardo da Vinci to Vesalius, were considered primarily as tools, despite their intrinsic artistic qualities. In their standard works, the major Renaissance architects, Serlio, Vignola, and Scamozzi tried to organize and systematize the remnants of the glorious pagan past. Their method was to clarify each detail as reliably as possible. They had, of course, Vitruvius' *De Architectura Libri Decem* in the backs of their minds. In some of their books, however, the title pages or chapter headings depict ancient ruins not with accuracy of detail, but as highly imaginative combinations of arches, columns, pedestals, obelisks, fragments of architraves, etc. Just because these infrequently appearing plates do not even pretend to offer closely measured descriptions of archeological value, they begin to appeal to us aesthetically in a way which the many archeologically accurate illustrations cannot achieve. Artists such as Heemskerck, Du Pérac, and Sadeler, in their freer and more naturalistic sketches and elaborate drawings of Roman ruins, were the first to emphasize the specific aesthetic value of ruins as such. They observed that neither Nature nor Art correspond entirely to rational and logical schemes, a fact which often bewildered systematically minded Renaissance thinkers.

But studying treatises and drawings of Roman antiquities was only one approach to the understanding and enjoyment of ruins. A still bigger audience—the public—became conscious of them through religious paintings in which ruins were employed as props for Biblical stories which had subjects as divergent as the Battle of Jericho and the Nativity. As the landscape in painting developed very slowly, from mere background illustration to subject matter of independent interest, so the ruin—originally only a casual prop in landscape painting—acquired a deeper meaning, and came to evoke a mood of its own, or even became a symbol.

Quite logically, the depiction of ruins in Italian painting of the early Renaissance depended to some degree on the continually progressing mastery of perspective. Thus, the technique of depicting the dilapidated stable in which Christ was born varies greatly from Filippo Lippi to Ghirlandajo and Botticelli and the modifications in perspective are as great as those in the clothing worn by the participants in the Nativity Scene.

The interest in and response to ruins played a much lesser role in the consciousness of central and northern Europeans. In the South—especially in Italy—ruins were always a familiar part of the daily physical environment, even though contemporary building styles were changing rapidly. In the North, by contrast, medieval architectural vernacular lingered on through the fifteenth and into the sixteenth century.

These traces of medievalism are perhaps most evident in the works of Hieronymus Bosch. But Pieter Breughel the Elder, who is the spiritual, but not stylistic heir to Bosch, belongs entirely to the Renaissance. Breughel absorbed Renaissance culture on his Italian travels, yet his paintings retain a distinctly northern quality of vision.

During the same two post-medieval centuries the ruin, even as a minor motif, appears even less frequently in Germany than in the Netherlands. There are exceptions in the so-called Donau School: Albrecht Altdorfer and Wolf Huber, for example. The greatest German master of this period, Albrecht Dürer shows very little interest in this motif, either in his paintings or in his graphic works. Occasionally, we see ruins in the backgrounds of his woodcuts and copper engravings. But they are without structural importance for the work as a whole, and count even less as emotional factors. This is true even in the well-known "Melancholia" (1514), a print which contains such a diversity of symbols.

If one considers Dürer's strongly rational bias, it is not surprising that to him, ruins were merely accessories. But the neglect of this motif by Matthias Grünewald is unexpected. This master, gifted with a macabre cosmic imagination, conjured up every conceivable sort of terrifying eeriness. He created a "machinery of horror" consisting of hellish flames, volcanoes, dead trees, demons, devils, witches, and fantastic monsters. But he never used the ruin to provoke horror and fear.

Fra Francesco Colonna

Hypnerotomachia Polifili *(Polifilo's Dream). The Polyandrion. 1499.*
Courtesy of the Cooper Union Museum, New York

This architectural-allegorical fairy tale, created about 1467 by this much-travelled Dominican monk, was published in Venice in 1499 by the famous printer Aldus Manutius. It is illustrated with 168 very suggestive woodcuts in which Love—sometimes depicted very realistically—and architecture are interwoven. In this bizarre fantasy Polifilo and his beloved move in hypnotic dream-like bewilderment through the ruins of an ancient temple—the Polyandrion.

In contrast with the plates found in sixteenth-century architectural treatises, the creator of the *Hypnerotomachia* is not interested in archeological details. Still less does he try to romanticize visual effects. He wants us to respond to space—to perceive every potential variation in three-dimensional forms. He tries to convey specific harmonies as they appear in architecture, in this case ruinous architecture.

QVINTO LIBRO D'ARCHITETTVRA,

DI SEBASTIAN SERLIO BOLOGNESE,

Nelquale fi tratta di diuerfe forme di Tempij facri, fecondo il
coftume Chriftiano, & al modo antico.

Con nuoua aggiunta delle mifure che feruono a tutti gli ordini de componimenti, che ui fi cotengono.

ROMA QVANTA FVIT IPSA RVINA DOCET

Sebastiano Serlio

Title Page of Book III of D'architettura. *Venice. 1540. Third
Edition 1551*

Serlio's treatise was the successor to those written by the Early Renaissance masters Leone Battista Alberti and Antonio Pietro Filarete. In turn, it became the prototype of the great architectural publications of the High Renaissance. Book III, devoted especially to Roman antiquities, contains drawings which are so carefully measured that they could be said to establish canons of architectural design. But in contrast the title page contains a woodcut which depicts an imaginary ancient arcade in a ruinous condition. There is a broken obelisk in the background, and fragments and columns are scattered about. Everything is overgrown with plants. This woodcut—an only slightly embellished, almost realistic combination of classical remainders—and the harmonious, well-balanced plates, show us that the rich emotional connotations of ruins were not yet appreciated. *Roma quanta fuit, ipsa ruina docet.* (Even ruins can teach what Rome once was.) What the artist of Serlio's time felt was sadness in the contemplation of the incompleteness and inevitable disintegration of all human works.

Pollio Marcus Vitruvius

Frontispiece from I Dieci Libri Dell'Architettura di M. Vitruvio
Tradutti et Commentati da Monsignor Barbaro Eletto Patriarca
D'Aquileggia. *In Vinegia Per Francesco Marcolini con Privileggi
MDLVI. Courtesy of the Cooper Union Museum, New York*

For many centuries, the basic works of the Roman architect Vitruvius exerted a strong influence. His *Ten Books on Architecture* survived the Middle Ages in manuscript form. They were published in the original Latin, together with German and Italian translations, beginning in the second half of the fifteenth century. Referred to again and again, Vitruvius was quoted as Bible and dogma. But each edition varied in details from the previous one, and these variations were indicative of the slightly different approach to architecture of each period.

In this 1556 edition, as in Serlio's treatise, the stylistic differences between the allegorical plates and those representing architecture *per se* is evident. Only on the frontispiece do we find a ruin, enlivened by human activities, made into a subject of topical interest. Sundials, pieces of construction machinery, and even musical instruments stress the connection between archeology, architecture, and the other arts. The whole is fused into a typical sixteenth-century pictorial paraphrase.

Compared with Serlio's title page, this woodcut is almost theatrical. Even the change from straight linear perspective to a kind of angular perspective contributes to this impression. Here, the unique charm of the ruin as such finds its expression, and in spite of the decayed condition of these monuments, the picture conveys no sad or negative feelings.

19

Wrangelschrank (Side Panel)

From Southern Germany. Dated 1566. Westfälisches Landesmuseum
für Kunst und Kulturgeschichte, Münster, Westphalia

This side panel from the so-called Wrangelschrank—a master-piece of South German cabinetmaking—is an especially charming example of the numerous adaptations of the ruin motif to the applied arts. Obviously, the ruin had been widely accepted as an interesting part of the physical landscape, although it was still generally thought to be inappropriate in a legitimate painting.

Here, the wooden panel is inlaid in intarsia (marquetry) work composed of multicolored wood such as maple, walnut, pear, plum, cherry, rose, lemon, and ebony—some of it natural, some artificially tinted. The "Rollwerk" (scrollwork)—at that time a popular German ornamental motif—is intertwined with arches, broken columns, and fragments of walls, as well as with fruit and small animals. However, it would be a mistake to give any symbolic interpretation to this intricate, merely decorative jumble of forms.

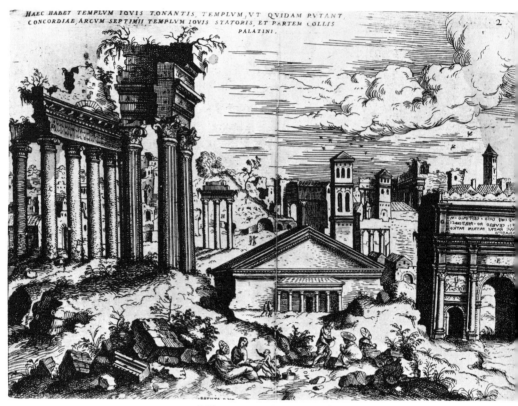

Vincenzo Scamozzi

Discorsi sull'Antichità di Roma. *Plate II. Venice. 1583*

Vincenzo Scamozzi, the last of the great Renaissance theoreticians of architecture, illustrated his *Discorsi* with engravings by
Giovanni Battista Pittoni the Elder. Pittoni had already published
these engravings in 1561 as *Praecipia Aliquot Romanae Antiquitatis
Ruinarum Monumenta.*

In this view of the Roman Forum, pieces of architecture such as
the columns of the Temple of Jupiter Tonans, of the Concordia
Temple, and of the Temple of Jupiter Stator, as well as a part of the
Arch of Septimius Severus are clearly recognizable, but their positions have been arbitrarily shifted.

Since the Renaissance, of course, this site has been further excavated, with the result that today much more of these buildings and
monuments can be seen. Their ruinous condition must have made a
stronger impression upon the observer of the sixteenth to eighteenth
centuries than it does upon the sightseer of today.

Pittoni wanted to achieve a naturalistic effect, so he inserted little
scenes of human interest, dramatic cloud formations, and scintillating
contrasts of light and shadow. He tried to reveal the unique characteristics of each piece of architecture. The result is a stimulating
catalogue-like compilation of the monuments which evokes archeological interest rather than giving aesthetic or emotional satisfaction.

Marten Van Heemskerck

Forum of Nerva. From Sketchbooks, *Volume II. Courtesy Foto-teca Unione, Rome*

In 1532, Marten van Heemskerck, the most outspoken of the early Dutch mannerists, went to Rome for a four-year stay. Precisely because he was a Northerner, and not brought up in the humanistic-archeological atmosphere of the South, his compositions sometimes have a greater sense of immediacy than those of his Italian contemporaries, who could only with difficulty escape from their classical erudition. Heemskerck's view of the Forum of Nerva, taken from his *Roman Sketch Books,* emphasizes the pictorial—almost the picturesque—more than archeological detail. This sketch almost gives these imposing monuments a feeling of friendliness and comfortable gentility.

Today, the columns on the right—the so-called Colonnacce—are completely above ground.

It is understandable that the Forum of Nerva has for centuries attracted the interest of artists. There is, for example, an anonymous drawing of it done in 1491—nearly fifty years before Heemskerck—in the Escorial collection, Madrid, and Piranesi made an etching of the Colonnacce about 1770.

Marten Van Heemskerck

Jericho. Plate VIII of the Clades. *The Metropolitan Museum of Art, Whittelsey Fund, 1960*

This artist from the Netherlands had an interest in ruins which was almost a mania, and which bore fruit in his later imaginary compositions. In "Clades, or Disasters of the Jewish Nation" engraved by his disciple Philip Galle, Heemskerck indulges his taste for picturesque ruins by depicting Old Testament catastrophes such as Jericho and Sodom. These engravings influenced Biblical illustration for years to come. They were imitated by the seventeenth-century Swiss engraver Matthaeus Merian—"Jericho" appears in "Samson Destroying the Temple of the Philistines." Merian's works were in turn plagiarized—with minor variations—throughout Europe.

Heemskerck's engravings in some ways anticipate Jacques Etienne Callot's seventeenth-century "Miseries of War," or Francisco Goya's nineteenth-century "Disasters of War." The difference between Heemskerck and these later artists is that they concentrate their attention and emotion on human suffering, whereas his interest lies in a more objective narrative. Heemskerck makes no attempt to create a freely imagined Biblical, or even a remotely Oriental-looking setting. His city of Jericho is composed of an amusing mixture of medieval and Roman ruins, for he wants to depict the ruinous state *per se*.

Etienne Du Pérac

Thermae of Caracalla. Drawing. Uffizi, Florence

The works of the Frenchman Etienne (Stefano) Du Pérac were for many years major sources for researchers in archeology. But his interest in subtle graphic work was at least as strong as that in achieving archeological exactitude.

This drawing of the Thermae of Caracalla shows that etching was Du Pérac's most natural form of artistic expression. This is also evidenced by his "Vestigi dell' Antichità di Roma" (1575). No wonder that he has often been called the predecessor of Piranesi (p. 128). But, although his more immediate approach makes his rendering appear much freer than that of other sixteenth-century masters, he still differs from Piranesi in his lack of emotional involvement with the subject matter.

The decayed condition of these buildings is persuasively conveyed. The drawing seems almost impressionistic compared with compositions by contemporaries such as Pittoni or G. A. Dosi. In any case, Du Pérac does not cram his sketch with archeological details. To read any specific emotion into it would be gratuitous speculation.

Egidius Sadeler

Nymphaeum Aquae Julia. Engraving *from* Vestigi della Antichità
di Roma Tivoli Pozzvolo e Altri Lvochi. *Plate XXV. Prague. 1606.
Courtesy of the Cooper Union Museum, New York*

We can see the extent of the changes which took place from the sixteenth to the seventeenth century in the visual interpretation of ruins if we compare this print by Sadeler—one of a set of fifty-two copper engravings—with sketches and engravings of Roman ruins by earlier artists.

At the beginning of the seventeenth century a major characteristic of Baroque appears: the heightened sensitivity to three-dimensional effects. This is recognizable in Sadeler's engraving of the Nymphaeum (built in the Age of Alexander Severus, 222-235 A.D.). The central part of the structure—the apse—is the focal point. It is framed by two arches, under which stand huge marble trophies. The apse is molded and emphasized by the strong antithesis of light and shadow, and by a parallel stress on the contrast of voids and volume in the substructure. It is unlikely that any sixteenth-century master would have considered the substructure essential to the overall impression of a ruin. But at the beginning of the Baroque period it was considered an intrinsic part of the whole. Even today the incomplete remnants of the Nymphaeum—both arches completely gone—are still impressive on the Piazza Vittorio Emanuele II in Rome.

To compare the representation of the ruins of the Nymphaeum with that of the Abbey of Heisterbach (p. 182) is worthwhile. Everything is different: the function—Nymphaeum and church, the style—Roman and late Romanesque, the ground plan, and the dimensions. Yet the three-dimensional treatment of space in both works produces a similar aesthetic effect.

Sandro Botticelli

The Adoration of the Magi. 1472-1473. National Gallery of Art, Washington, D. C. Andrew Mellon Collection

During the Quattrocento, the difference between archeological and aesthetic interest was not yet clearly felt. Even today, the sophisticated sightseers who visit the Roman Forum do not always make the appropriate distinction between these two approaches to ruins.

When ruined buildings first appeared in paintings—about the middle of the fifteenth century—there was no interest in the structure as such; only in its condition of decay; as something which emphasized the humble, impoverished surroundings of Christ's birth.

Botticelli, like his contemporaries, built his ruin out of fragments of classical architecture and connected these pieces by wooden beams. The tumble-down stable became a stage setting—the center of the composition.

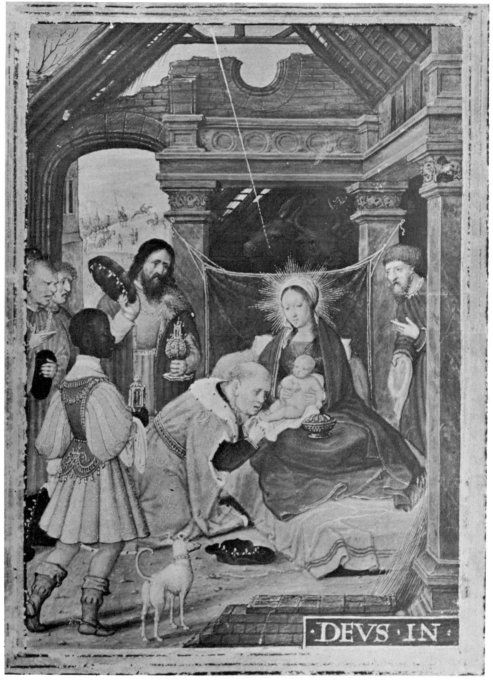

The Adoration of the Magi

Page from the Sforza Book of Hours *(Flemish Miniatures and Borders: ca. 1519). The British Museum, London*

About the beginning of the fifteenth century, the use of classical ruins as settings for the Nativity and the Adoration of the Magi spread from Italy to the North. The Italian artists were stimulated by the presence of Greek and Roman ruins, whereas northerners were not exposed to this influence. So it is all the more remarkable that ruins appeared in works such as this one. Here, the artist was obviously fascinated by patterns of brickwork, and we can clearly see the minute rendering of the brick walls. This specific interest in brickwork is already found in manuscripts which date from the sixth century on. Here, the ruin merely provides a frame, whereas in Botticelli's "Adoration" it is the focal point.

Albrecht Altdorfer

The Birth of Christ. 1512. Staatliche Museen, Gemäldegalerie,
Berlin

Ruins have always appeared more frequently in Italian than in German and Netherlandish paintings. Nevertheless, some northern artists such as Albrecht Altdorfer, the most impressive painter to come out of the so-called Donau (Danube) School, created fascinating studies of ruins. Many medieval and Renaissance paintings contain Nativity scenes which take place in shabby dilapidated-looking buildings. Nevertheless these dreary edifices, which merely look as though they need the services of a carpenter, never give the impact of a genuine ruin. For example, although Rogier van der Weyden's "Adoration of the Magi" (ca. 1450) influenced later German versions of the same theme, his shed-like structure is only one of many background elements.

Altdorfer, however, gives the shelter for the Holy Family depth and complexity, and in fact makes it the central content matter of the picture. There are sharp contrasts of light and shadow and an almost surrealistic surface treatment. The overall impression is romantic, picturesque, and fairytale-like. The mood is that of "Gemütlichkeit"—a radical change from the eerie quality of his earlier (1507) treatment of the same subject. If we compare the brickwork in Altdorfer's painting with that of the Sforza manuscript, the developments taking place in the rendering of ruins become evident.

Hieronymus Bosch

Hell. Wing from the Hay-Wain. Prado, Madrid

It is difficult to imagine Bosch as a contemporary of Botticelli. For Bosch, the burning or burnt-out ruin, surrounded by flames, becomes synonymous with hell—a symbol of heavenly punishment, fear, terror, and torture. Bosch's ruins, here as well as in his "Last Judgment" and "Temptation of Saint Anthony" convey the same medieval feeling of anguish and oppression; the ever-present sense of sin and guilt mirrored by the great works of Romanesque and Gothic sculpture.

Bosch's singleness of vision is much stronger than the faint remnants of the medieval tradition which still lingered on in the Netherlands of his time.

He obviously enjoys the telling of the story with elaborate details. In this work, the ruins are as important to the plot as the figures—these half-freaks, half-monsters with meager limbs and angular movements. We are not, of course, interested in the architectural forms of the ruins: their ghastliness alone is sufficient to hold our attention.

Pieter Breughel the Elder

The Tower of Babel. 1563. Kunsthistorisches Museum, Vienna

Of all that man constructs, the naked brick building by the look of its material appears most like a ruin. Like a ruin, it displays its essential structural elements. Like a torso in sculpture it may or may not convey an aesthetic impression. The story of the Tower of Babel (Genesis XI) has been depicted frequently and with different degrees of skill and persuasiveness in medieval manuscripts, and as late as the fifteenth century in the Duke of Bedford's *Hours,* and in the *Grimani Breviary.* In this and in his other versions of the Tower of Babel, Breughel combines the "not yet" with the "no longer"; the part in *statu nascendi* with the completed section. But the completed section is already falling away. The "Tower of Babel" is symbolic of man's delusion that he can reach the heavens, and of the curse which accompanies his attempts to achieve this dream. Using a highly original combination of chromatic and graphic elements, Breughel depicts this eternal human tragedy by presenting a multitude of minute and varied details drawn from everyday life.

El Greco

View of Toledo. Ca. 1600. The Metropolitan Museum of Art, Bequest of Mrs. H. O. Havemeyer, 1929. The H. O. Havemeyer Collection

Sometimes half-dreams, vague as they are, in some mysterious way sink into the mind, stimulating the imagination, intensifying sensitivities, and deepening emotions. El Greco's "Toledo," a city which seems ready to be devoured or consumed, affects us in this way. It is as though the artist had chosen his colors with the intention of conveying every possible nuance of disintegration.

Toledo in the time of El Greco was actually a very vital city, and in another painting the great Spanish mannerist presents it in a more realistic way, even sketching details of buildings and topography for an accompanying map. But here, we only feel the shock of impending catastrophe. Even the landscape is menacing and oppressive. The effect is that of the immediacy of decay in a setting of ominous solitude. As words can take on different meanings in different contexts, so the familiar, everyday appearance of the buildings of Toledo acquires a tragic face—that of doomed ruins. The artist has miraculously transformed a prosperous community into a scene of desolation which seems to be ready for the next stage: that of total dissolution.

But are these really ruins? For El Greco's method is not the usual one of displaying half-destroyed forms or chaotic accumulations of stones. Instead, he uses the ingenious device of changing the actual positions of structures such as the cathedral and the bridge into bizarre irregularity. Even more decisively, he turns most of the structures around, so that in their frontal view they seem to be completely flat and without depth, like wings on a stage; and even more remote from the stream of life than real ruins.

The
Seventeenth
and Eighteenth
Centuries in
Italy and France
and the
Echo in the North

The Seventeenth and Eighteenth Centuries in France and Italy and The Echo in the North

In early sixteenth-century painting—in contrast to the graphic arts—the depiction of ancient ruins is still relatively rare. But in the seventeenth century they gradually became a subject for painters throughout Europe. By then, most northern artists had become familiar with the monuments of antiquity, for they had either seen them represented in woodcuts or copper engravings, or had visited the actual sites in Italy.

The impact of Italy on the northern-European artist cannot be overemphasized. His soul was divided between his longing for that country whose art and life he idolized and idealized, and natural attachment to the artistic traditions of his own land. In his eyes, Italy was almost synonymous with Rome and the Roman Campagna, which in turn meant Roman ruins. An Italianizing school arose, for example, in Holland, different from the school of the Flemish "Romanists" which had begun in the early sixteenth century.

Roman ruins were characteristic motifs in the works of the French-born seventeenth-century masters Claude Lorrain and Nicolas Poussin. Both men were Italianized to such a degree that their paintings became prototypes of the sort of "classical" composition in which the ruin motif becomes dominant. Landscape and monumental architecture are more intimately connected in the works of Claude Lorrain than in those of Poussin.

Salvator Rosa was the most famous landscapist of the age. He was a painter, a poet, and a musician, and his influence upon the arts was felt throughout Europe during the seventeenth and eighteenth centuries. He often enriched his landscapes with fantastic ruins, but in a way entirely different from Poussin and Claude Lorrain and the Italianizing Dutch and Flemish Schools. Salvator Rosa's paintings were chiefly responsible for the fact that the image of ruins became a fad and fashion among European art collectors.

The paintings of the Neapolitan Desiderio F. Monsù appear to be excessively dramatic compared with those of Salvator Rosa and

47

the masters whom Rosa influenced. They seem to mirror an unbridled fantasy; an entirely private and unique imaginative world, thus creating new emotional effects.

Generally, the seventeenth century saw a tremendous increase in the general interest in ruins. Poetry, travel diaries, and letters also showed a fascination with this odd and ambiguous motif. However, it is not our task here to juxtapose literary and visual developments.

During the eighteenth century, the enthusiastic preoccupation with ruins turned into a mania. This theme, an emotional heritage of the preceding century, remained no longer restricted to painting and the graphic arts—now it embraced all of the applied arts, from textiles to wallpaper; from ceramics to the goldsmiths' craft. Perhaps most important, artificial ruins began to occupy a place in landscaping. Yet, in spite of its employ in the applied arts, the ruin motif was still more significant in the painting and graphic arts of that period. For example, ruins are the focal points in the works of masters such as Pannini, Piranesi, and Hubert Robert. But their interpretations are so different—visually, emotionally, and psychologically—that they are better discussed in connection with "Classicism."

Sebastiano Ricci and Alessandro Magnasco, both Venetians, were born a generation earlier than Pannini. Their works also reflect the increasing interest in ruins; an interest which, however, did not elevate them into a major motif. These men were stylistically and imaginatively dissimilar, but they both used an outspoken baroque idiom. The attitude toward ruins of Sebastiano Ricci was like that of many of his contemporaries: they were too often used merely as conventional props. But, unlike his less-gifted contemporaries, his visual phraseology is so inventive and pleasing, that neither the broken columns, nor the fragments of ancient buildings can divert the spectator's attention from the pseudo-heroic central theme.

Magnasco's demonic fantasies reflect the transition from the seventeenth to the eighteenth century in a different way. Like his predecessor and fellow Neapolitan Desiderio Monsù, he strove to create an effect of spontaneity. So his works have a freer, more eighteenth than seventeenth-century spirit. The violent conflict between light and shadow accentuates the severe outlines of Magnasco's ruins, and gives his scenes—mythological and religious alike—a theatrical effect.

Whether one should call Magnasco's ruins "romantic" is a question of semantics. The ruin lends itself so strongly to romantic interpretation that a satisfactory aesthetic definition of Romanticism could be formulated by referring only to ruins in literature and the visual arts. The paradox that something which strictly speaking should belong to death should also make its presence felt in the realm of life, was to become a favorite obsession of the nineteenth-century romantics. Even before the end of the seventeenth century, the visual representation of ruins occasionally conveyed an outspokenly romantic mood. For example, Jacob Ruisdael and Rembrandt can in no way be called "romantic" painters. Nevertheless, they left behind certain works in which ruins are instrumental in evoking romantic feelings.

It is strange that so many artists from Venice, a city which had no direct ties with antiquity, were receptive to the visual and emotional impact of the glories of the past. The ruins which appear in the works of Canaletto and Guardi prove that such awareness did exist. The trembling, vibrant luminosity in their drawings and paintings—especially Guardi, who was one of the last great geniuses of Italian painting—fused ruins, real or imaginary, to the atmosphere of Venice. It was not, of course, just the Venetian painters who brought about these changes. The spirit of the eighteenth century, radiating from France, affected all of European painting. Form and matter were dissolved. The impact of massy shapes lost its importance, and space began to flow. Light enveloped everything, and profuse ornamentation replaced the multiple rhythms of baroque composition. Stone, wood, and fabrics seemed to dematerialize, and spatial unity was stressed more than the representation of particular architectural components.

Nicolas Poussin

Ruins of an Arch of Triumph. Musée, Rennes

Translating emotion into reason, and intuition into ordered law, the "classicist" Poussin, who made Rome his adopted home, subordinated landscape, architecture, and the human figure to the organization of space. Architecture to him was synonymous with ruins, and ruins always meant to him ruins of classical antiquity. In his geometrically-organized landscapes, ruins serve as three-dimensional checking points, like the houses in a Cézanne landscape, which establish a harmonious balance in depth, although he builds his landscape layer by layer and plane by plane. Heroic dignity dictates the underlying pattern of horizontals and verticals into which fall trees, bushes, and human figures, together with the never precisely identifiable columns and arches of his Roman ruins. And for this sometimes rather academic scheme, it makes no difference whether the story is mythological or religious, or merely a genre scene. The design, purified from the virus of life, is decisive—especially in his paintings, less so in his sketches. What a contrast to Desiderio or even to Salvator Rosa!

Claude Gellée (called Lorrain)

Roman Forum. 1633-1634. Courtesy Museum of Fine Arts, Springfield, Mass.

The major difference between Claude Lorrain and his contemporary, compatriot, and fellow classicist Poussin is that Lorrain is more concerned with light, color, and atmosphere, values not too frequently encountered in seventeenth-century painting outside the Netherlands. Lorrain created many works in which stately, dignified architecture provides the setting for stories taken from the Bible or from classical mythology. There are others, which he calls "Caprices," in which landscape and ruin, instead of intact architecture, combine to create an ensemble of great poetic charm—"well taught to counterfeit the waste of time." Lorrain's ruins are often real Roman monuments such as the Colosseum, groups of columns on the Forum, porticoes, and temples; all of which he had previously studied and sketched. Sometimes he intersperses fantastic variations and free inventions with these authentic structures. The *Liber Veritatis,* a collection of about two hundred drawings which the artist made after his own paintings, shows clearly the goals of his art: the world he dreamed of. The poetic and lyrical qualities of the scene are emphasized through the diffusion of light and the variety of nuances in color, as are the architectural elements themselves. The calm radiance of light, which even permeates the irregular forms of the ruins, softens the formality and rigidity of the underlying scheme. And so do the figures of humans and animals which enliven the scene. They remind us that the Forum Romanum was once the Campo Vaccino (cow meadow). Lorrain's ruined buildings are closely fused with the natural surroundings. So ruins and Nature contribute equally to the totality of our visual experience. When Goethe solemnly stated "In Claude Lorrain erklärt Natur sich für ewig" (In Claude Lorrain, Nature declares itself eternal), he was perhaps not aware that one of the reasons for this impression was the presence of ruins.

Pierre Lemaire (called Lemaire-Poussin)

Ancient Corner of the Forum. Collection Professor Briganti, Rome

Out of friendship with the artist, the painter and engraver Pierre Lemaire added to his name the surname of Nicolas Poussin. This was very appropriate indeed, for Lemaire's paintings are more "poussinesque" than the originals. Lemaire's works give the impression of having come more from humanistic erudition than from immediate visual experience. His ruins are tasteful combinations of ancient monuments, but they lack force and depth of feeling. As a less-gifted artist often tends to exaggerate the salient characteristics of his subject matter, so Lemaire-Poussin overloads his paintings with relics. The juxtaposition with Poussin's work will show by contrast the serene organization of landscape and ruin achieved by the latter.

Salvator Rosa

Shipwreck with Ruins. Galleria Estense, Modena.
Photo, Gabinetto Fotografico Nazionale, Rome

Salvator Rosa, painter, poet, and musician, was largely responsible for making ruins a fad among artists, poets, scholars, collectors, and even in bourgeois circles. One hundred years later, Horace Walpole, creator of Strawberry Hill, considered Rosa to be one of the greatest painters of all time. Rosa had a profound influence upon English visual art, and upon the erudite Englishman's way of looking at nature. It is difficult to imagine an eighteenth-century English landscaped park without artificial ruins. And these ruins always look as though they had been taken from a painting by Salvator Rosa. One could almost say that he discovered the "picturesque" before it became a trend. He was courageous enough to look at nature in a new way; to stress its more terrifying aspects which were best symbolized by ruins. Rosa's vision is closely allied with concrete visual experience; it is not macabre or theatrical, like that of Desiderio: the ruins in Rosa's paintings are like signposts which lead the beholder to participation in the emotions which the artist wants him to feel. This approach gives to Rosa's landscapes that quality of persuasiveness which made them an influence upon so many generations of painters and landscapists.

Monsù Desiderio

Ruins. Venice, Private Collection

About one-and-a-half centuries after its appearance as a mere prop, the ruin became a legitimate subject for painting in the hands of artists such as the Neapolitan Desiderio and Salvator Rosa (p. 56). Until then, mannerists and early baroque artists had looked at ruins primarily as objects upon which they could display their skill in manipulating light and shadow; color and tonal values. Like most seventeenth-century artists, Desiderio wanted to capture the architectural variety of columns, architraves, aedicula, reliefs, and occasional Gothic forms. But he was still more fascinated by images of destruction and decay. The religious or mythological stories with their dream-like atmosphere, theatrical settings, and human figures, which are contained in his paintings are irrelevant. The accent is upon a more or less disorderly collection of ruins, and upon the fantastic perspectives of avenues and piazzas. It would be misleading, however, to label Desiderio's works as either romantic or picturesque, for there is no direct appeal to the emotions of the beholder. His paintings are basically spectacles, even though they are raised to the highest artistic plane.

Antonio Travi

Pastorale. Collection Renzo Rava, New York

Thus far, the examples of ruins in painting have been selected from artists who were outstanding in their generation. The Genoese Travi cannot be placed in this category. He is included because he shows how the ruin has also become a subject of interest to less-gifted artists, and that this macabre theme is gaining a wider audience. Travi concentrates all means of composition and color on the background: an aspect of painting which had been neglected for centuries. He makes the erratic forms and raw brickwork of an unidentifiable building convey a mood of despair—but it is despair which does not interfere with the "pastorale" in the foreground. In spite of the somber, sinister quality of this canvas, it differs totally from the depth, mystery, and demonic eeriness of Desiderio, who was Travi's senior by only one generation.

Paul Brill

Roman Landscape with Ruins and Forum. Herzog Anton Ulrich-Museum, Braunschweig

Like many other northern painters, the Fleming Paul Brill went to Rome, arriving in 1574 and remaining there until his death. One would assume that steady exposure to Roman architecture and countryside would have influenced his work, but it did not. Although his landscapes are filled with Roman ruins, the atmosphere has a distinctly northern, non-Mediterranean sharpness to it. The ruins look obtrusive—like stage props. The minute, delineated figures of humans and animals are more important to the artist than the monuments of the past. If we compare this painting to a similar bucolic scene by van Poelenburgh (p. 64), we see even more clearly that Brill's ruins are merely clumsy additions, while in van Poelenburgh there is a harmonious balance of nature and architecture.

Cornelis van Poelenburgh

Roman Landscape. The Toledo Museum of Art, Toledo, Ohio.
Gift of Edward Drummond Libbey

Since the end of the sixteenth century, northern European artists have expressed their longing for Italy through literature and the visual arts. They were affected by two stimuli: the direct experience of the sunlight and clarity of the Italian landscape, and the presence of ancient traditions. The "Romanist" Flemish and Dutch painters, called "De Bentveughels" (migratory birds) were first impressed by imported Italian prints and pieces of applied art. But they soon flocked to Rome, where their reaction to antiquity was very different from that of Heemskerck, whose interest a hundred years earlier was mainly archeological (p. 24). The changes taking place in European painting appear in van Poelenburgh's treatment of landscape, living figures, colors, light, and above all in his ruins. These ruins seem to be an integral part of the processes of nature, but they are never terrifying or tragic. Even more than the earlier Romanists such as Adam Elsheimer, Gillis van Coninxloo, and Paul Brill, van Poelenburgh chooses to depict the idyllic aspects of buildings in decay, very different from the heroic approach of the French classicists Poussin and Claude Lorrain (p. 52). As with other Romanists, certain qualities of northern painting, especially realistic details, remain in van Poelenburgh's works, but these are subordinated to the uniquely Italian aesthetic combination of nature and history. And ruins make a major contribution to this harmony.

Aelbert Cuyp

Ubbergen Castle. The Tate Gallery, London

The combination of a wide landscape and figures of humans or cattle in the foreground distinguishes Cuyp's oeuvre from that of the majority of his Dutch contemporaries such as Ruisdael and Hobbema. The ruin is part of the landscape, and the persons in the foreground are motivated as interested spectators. This painting has a greater variety of rich, deep colors, and is more suffused with light than the usual seventeenth-century Dutch landscape. Understandably, Cuyp has been called the Dutch Claude Lorrain. At first glance, this lovely view of a Dutch castle set against the scenery of the lower Rhine seems romantic; comparable to works of the early nineteenth century. But further study shows that there is nothing about it which is "romantic" in the sense of being emotional or highly personal.

Jacob van Ruisdael

The Cemetery. 1655-1660. The Detroit Institute of Arts, Detroit, Michigan

No landscape painted at the height of Romanticism could be more "romantic" than this one. Here are barren trees, waterfalls, threatening-looking clouds, and ruins. These elements cannot be encountered in van Ruisdael's other works, nor are they stressed in the paintings of his Dutch contemporaries. For they, too, prefer more sedate, non-romantic subjects such as quiet streams, dense forests, peaceful fields, and leafy, isolated trees. Van Ruisdael is not interested in the architecture of these ruins—he uses them merely as a vehicle to convey a mood of sadness, death, and decay. They are to remind the onlooker of the transience of worldly things, comparable to the so-called Vanitas still lifes of contemporary Spanish masters like Antonio Pereda and Valdés Leal. The somber atmosphere, as well as the subject matter of Ruisdael's canvas is unique in seventeenth-century Dutch landscape painting. There is an interplay of light and shadow with luminous forms which have a strong three-dimensional quality, in some ways surprisingly like those formed by John Constable, the English master to whom ruins were also of major importance (p. 186).

The works of Rembrandt, Ruisdael's greatest contemporary, will not be discussed here, for on the rare occasions in which ruins appear on Rembrandt's canvas, they have little emotional or symbolic importance.

Sebastiano and Marco Ricci

Memorial to Admiral Sir Clowdisley Shovell. 1723-1729. National Gallery of Art, Washington, D. C. Samuel H. Kress Collection

The Venetians Sebastiano Ricci and his younger brother Marco used ruins to enliven dull subject matter. Both men were rather competent artists, who often worked together; Marco doing the landscape and architecture and Sebastiano filling in the live figures. In this way they painted some of the most charming works to come out of the Venetian School in the early eighteenth century. The Riccis stripped ruins of all historical, archeological, and emotional associations, leaving only decorative values. They were so skillful and inventive that our attention is never distracted by the fragments of buildings or by the broken columns: the eye is drawn immediately to the pseudo-heroic central theme.

It was their vivacity and eye for the theatrical which prevented the Riccis from turning out pedantic, catalogue-like, empty baroque allegories; for all the then-usual trite ingredients are present. The appearance of ruins in this sort of allegory marks the beginning of their degradation from a meaningful symbol to a piece of superficial decoration.

Eugene Mac Swiny

Tombeaux Des Princes Des Grands Capitaines. *Paris. 1737-1738.*
Tomb of Lord Shovell, engraved by N. Tardieu and D. M. Fratta,
after S. and M. Ricci. Courtesy of The Cooper Union Museum,
New York

About 1725, Eugene Mac Swiny, an impresario, organized the execution of a memorial to commemorate famous British heroes in allegorical paintings. Mac Swiny dictated the style of these paintings down to the last detail. He commissioned only Venetian painters, and had the paintings shipped from Venice to England, where they were engraved. It is interesting that in the engravings the architectural details show up more clearly than in the paintings, for the ruins were intended to be only a kind of accompanying music. See page 70.

Alessandro Magnasco

*The Martyrdom of St. Erasmus. First half Eighteenth Century.
Collection Ulderico Tononi, Milan*

(PLEASE REFER TO PAGE 76)

74

Church of St. Aegidien, Nürnberg

Built in 1140, reconstructed in 1711-1718, destroyed in World War II. Photograph, Bildarchiv Foto, Marburg

(PLEASE REFER TO PAGE 77)

75

Alessandro Magnasco

Ruins are elements essential to the paintings of the Genoese Magnasco, active in Milan. Most of his French and Italian contemporaries used ruins only to enrich and enliven their canvases. The human figures in Magnasco's scenes are small, and are always dominated by the background, whether natural or architectural. He depicted interiors of monasteries and hermitages, gypsy camps, roving soldiers, and Biblical and mythological stories. There is a contrast between his sweeping, spontaneous, almost impressionistic brushstroke and the solidity of the architecture which frames the scene. The monuments and buildings always look solid, even when they are half-disintegrated. Magnasco fluctuated between two styles: Baroque and Rococo; between the Italian and the Spanish traditions. The architecture has a rhetorical, grandiloquent quality; the gestures of the human figures are exaggerated; disquieting.

St. Erasmus was supposedly martyred in 303 A.D., during the reign of Diocletian, and the architecture in the painting is basically true to that era. But the artist cannot refrain from adding some high baroque anachronisms such as the Tiepolesque angels.

Church of St. Aegidien, Nürnberg

The actual architectural forms of this bombed-out cathedral are similar to the vision of spatial sequences in Magnasco's "Martyrdom of St. Erasmus" (p. 74). The arches, borrowed elements of Roman baroque, and the round architraves without cupolas are almost identical. The cupola of St. Aegidien's is completely gone, while in Magnasco's painting it is concealed by celestial clouds which are enlivened by delightful little angels. The feeling of ruins is stronger in Magnasco's art than in the realism of the photograph. Magnasco achieves this effect largely by skillful use of space.

Alessandro Magnasco in Collaboration with Clemente Spera

Bacchanal Among Ruins. Collection, R. and B. Suida Manning, New York

As in his "Martyrdom of St. Erasmus," Magnasco makes the architecture fit the story. These magnificent ruins monumentalize the idyllic scene and create an atmosphere of an idealized Grecian past. They become even more poetic through the creeping foliage.

Giovanni Antonio Canaletto

Basilica of St. Maxentius. First half Eighteenth Century.
Milan. Collection, Campanini-Bonomi

Three facts may explain the particular sensitivity to colors; their nuances and tonal values, which distinguishes Venetian painters from other Italian schools: Venice was the gateway for the import of exotic articles such as elaborate, richly colored Oriental carpets, fabrics, and tiles. In addition, her artists inherited the Byzantine tradition of glowing colors. And most important, her atmosphere had (and of course still has) the peculiarity that mist and moisture break light into brilliant prismatic refractions. The oeuvre of Giovanni Antonio Canaletto should be carefully distinguished from that of his less-gifted nephew, pupil, and imitator Bernardo Bellotto, also called Canaletto.

Giovanni Antonio sold his works to erudite European and English travellers who wanted souvenirs of the "Grand Tour." Connoisseurs and collectors, men of exquisite taste and discernment, like Horace Walpole, praised his works both for their aesthetic qualities and for their topographical reliability. When in the early 1740's Canaletto went to Rome, he gave new lustre and a warm, golden atmosphere to ruins which had already been drawn, etched, and painted so many times. Since there had never been any noteworthy ruins in Venice, he was all the more fascinated by these relics of an earlier past than Venice could offer.

Quite understandably, his views of London, painted a few years after the Venetian scenes, lack the luminous qualities of the latter, while retaining their wonderful accuracy of representation.

Francesco Guardi

*Fantastic Landscape. The Metropolitan Museum of Art, Bequest of
Mrs. H. O. Havemeyer, 1929. The H. O. Havemeyer Collection*

In Francesco Guardi's oeuvre, the ruins have no deep emotional, historical, or moral meaning: they are like the flowers or oyster shells in a still life. But to describe his ruins as strictly decorative would be misleading. As in abstract painting, the subject matter is of secondary importance, and our attention is drawn by the brilliant, whirling colors. Ruins gave Guardi the perfect subject upon which to exercise the playful magic of his brush. We see how reality was incapable of imposing limitations upon the freedom and subjectivity of this wizard of the palette.

Guardi was a pupil of Canaletto (p. 80), and was deeply influenced by him. Guardi's works also reveal techniques found in paintings by Giovanni Battista Tiepolo (p. 86), the greatest Venetian painter of that century, by Pannini (p. 122), and by Magnasco (p. 74). But the unusual brush stroke, the scintillating colors, the loose fragments, and the kaleidoscopic effects of light and shadow are entirely Guardi's. The gaiety and extravagance of Venetian life is mirrored in his paintings with the same vividness that we experience in the theater of Goldoni and Gozzi, as well as in Casanova's autobiography. Guardi's "vedute" and "capricci" should be seen in the original, for black and white cannot convey the effortless quality of his technique. The "Fantastic Landscape" gives the effect of luminosity, weightlessness and unreality: a mood which pervades the entire canvas: sky, sea, boats, monuments, and ruins.

Francesco Guardi

Classical Ruins in a Landscape. (Capriccio). Fogg Art Museum,
Harvard University

For Guardi, ruins are shimmering, ephemeral combinations of forms and changing colors, never objects of archeological interest. He occasionally pays lip service to the rather sober spirit of approaching Neoclassicism, but in this painting he transforms the architecture into something resembling a gay, bubbling rococo centerpiece with an almost impressionistic dematerialization of forms.

Giovanni Battista Tiepolo

*The Adoration of the Magi. Sketch. Mid-eighteenth Century. The
Metropolitan Museum of Art, Rogers Fund, 1937*

There is a great difference in the aesthetic function of the ruin between the charming, graceful vistas of Canaletto (p. 80) or Guardi (p. 82), and the frescoes, ceiling paintings, and canvases executed by Tiepolo. The latter ingeniously combines very dramatic composition with convincing illusionistic effects. His color scheme— entirely eighteenth-century—is bright and fresh, and moreover his work is always extremely decorative. Tiepolo was highly regarded throughout Europe, and his many works are scattered throughout Italy, though the majority remain in Venetian churches and palaces. The ceilings and murals which he painted especially for the castles in Würzburg and Madrid gave him an international reputation. There is always an impression of fleeting movement; of transience in heaven and on earth, but this transience in no way diminishes the grandeur of the scene. Even in this small sketch, Tiepolo fortifies the composition by incorporating large pieces of intact architecture or dilapidated ruinous parts. His ruins are always festive; never tragic or sentimental. The perfect integration of the vertical columns and the curve of the triumphal arch with the graceful movements of the human figures is characteristic of his well-organized narrative style, as is his uninhibited use of a piece of ancient architecture as footstool for the Virgin.

APPLIED ARTS

Service De L'Accouchée

Faïence, Italy. Pesaro (?) about 1760. Courtesy of the Cooper Union Museum, New York

It is amusing to encounter ruins which decorate objects as heterogeneous as these. Here, the ruin is accompanied by the equally popular urn motif. The design is repeated three times: on the tureen, on a large cup, and on the cover of a typical *service de l'accouchée*. These sets were used by fashionable eighteenth-century society to have meals served at bedside. The material is glazed faïence from one of the famous Italian factories where this sort of ceramic had been made since the sixteenth century. Until the development of porcelain in the eighteenth century, these faïences were highly valued by connoisseurs, and found their way into many elegant European homes. The overglaze decoration is similar to the Venetian "vedutas" by Canaletto and Guardi (pp. 80, 82). The faïence painters, who considered themselves to be artisans rather than artists, liked to play about with these popular motifs, without troubling themselves about serious connotations.

Nymphenburg Porcelain

Fountain Grotto. German. 1765-1775. Allen Art Museum, Oberlin
College, Oberlin, Ohio

In the eighteenth century, the ruin motif was so popular that it invaded almost all of the decorative arts. This occurred even when the proportions and materials used were completely out of harmony with those of a ruin which was to serve as model. Polite society, accustomed to seeing artificial ruins in its parks and gardens, also wanted to enjoy them in the porcelain objects which enlivened the interiors of their houses as ornaments. Of course, this delicately executed piece of an elaborate table decoration reduces the scale of an artificial ruin. It also changes the traditional grouping of grotto and ruin as background for a fountain into an even more playful combination of swinging "rocaille" forms. The use of typical rococo pastel tones, with no attempt to imitate nature, completes the metamorphosis.

This lovely piece originated in the Bavarian court manufactory, which was founded in 1758 in Nymphenburg. It is attributed to one of the most outstanding sculptors in porcelain, Franz Anton Bustelli. It is a triumphant manifestation of the rococo spirit, which could transform subjects like ruins—generally associated with the macabre—into gay bric-a-brac.

English Cotton, The Old Ford (detail)

Late Eighteenth Century. English version with signature of Jones, 1761. Courtesy of the Cooper Union Museum, New York

Fabrics used for curtains, drapes, upholstery, etc. were important in the decorative arts of the eighteenth century. When materials such as silk and damask were too expensive, cotton and chintzes printed with decorative motifs were used instead. These motifs were sometimes ornamental, sometimes narrative. The subject matter had to be pleasing and easy to understand. This pastoral scene is taken from an etching by Nicholas Berchem, dated 1652. The peacock and poultry are from an engraving which in turn stems from a seventeenth-century painting by Marmaduke Cradock published in London in 1740. The Roman ruins and later architectural fragments are capriciously interspersed. The thread which binds the ruin to Rome or to medieval Europe has been lost.

French Toile De Jouy

Scene from Don Quixote *(detail). Ca. 1785. Courtesy of the Cooper Union Museum, New York*

French arts and crafts of the eighteenth century were often enriched by German artisans. In 1758 a German immigrant named Wilhelm Philipp Oberkampf founded a textile mill in Jouy, near Versailles. He was under the patronage of the King of France, who wanted to compete with the cotton products which the English were marketing. Ruins merely add charm to this little scene from Cervantes' masterwork; they have no inner connection with it.

Crèche with the Adoration of the Shepherds and the Kings

From Innsbruck. Mid-eighteenth Century.
Bavarian National Museum, Munich

Crèches were carved and painted representations of the Nativity. They first appeared at the end of the Middle Ages, and became popular in Central Europe during the seventeenth and eighteenth centuries. They resembled miniature stage settings, and were populated by humans and animals. They were shown in both city and country. Although influenced by the Passion Play, crèches were of course less solemn, and usually contained sentimental genre scenes and amusing byplay. They are still exhibited in Bavaria and in the Tyrol, and occasionally in Italy and Spain, and are seen at Christmas in churches, monasteries, and in Catholic homes, helping to keep traditions of folklore alive. The Neapolitan Giuseppe Sammartino was the most famous carver of crèches, but other baroque artists such as the Bavarian sculptor Ignaz Günther also made them. Here, the ruin is a variation of the familiar humble stable. The mood is astonishingly like that of Altdorfer's "Nativity," which was created over two centuries before this tableau (p. 36). There is an aura of the cozy privacy of the family circle in spite of the presence of the Three Kings. The ruined building suggests neither decay nor misery: it is merely the shelter for Mother and Child.

STAGE DESIGN

Stage Design

Stage design certainly contributed as much to the increasing interest in ruins as did the development in painting. Theater and opera, and the closely related art of stage design reached their climax in the seventeenth and eighteenth centuries. Small wonder that painting, the graphic arts, sculpture, and architecture acquired the qualities of the baroque stage—a sense of movement, exaggeration, accumulation of spatial effects, and, of course, dramatization—in short, Baroque.

Stylistic expression during the Baroque period had split into two directions: into the Berninesque and the Palladian classicist Baroque, and this division was especially evident in stage design. Palladio, in his famous Teatro Olimpico, which he built in Vicenza in 1582, and which is still almost intact, constructed scenes in a sort of three-dimensional relief perspective, unmovable and unchangeable.

The "telari," first used in Mantua in 1598, made the changing of the set possible. They were prism-shaped devices which turned upon an axle and this way permitted the use of three different sets. Through the writings of the German architect Joseph Furttenbach and especially through his *Architectura Civilis* (Ulm, 1628) we learn about the devices of the "telari" stage and about the technique of changing theatrical sets with which he had become acquainted in Italy as a pupil of Giulio Parigi (p. 104). The next, and most decisive step in the development of stage setting was the invention of wings by Giovanni Battista Aleotti. Until the nineteenth century, wings remained the only technical device for changing sets. Aleotti's invention finally enabled stage designers to create according to the dictates of their fantasy. Illumination, fireworks, aerial machinery, artificial waterfalls, and other technical "miracles" soon were employed on the stage and, among a wealth of new motifs, ruins also began to appear. After some experimental attempts of amateurs like the performance of Ottavio Rinuccini's *Dafne,* 1595, the first true opera, Claudio Monteverdi's *Orfeo* had been performed in Venice in 1607, and it has always been the "grand opera" which stimulated the art of stage design most intensely. To the seventeenth-or eighteenth-century spectator the set was at least as important—often more so—than the plot or music. This emphasis of the visual aspects of the stage is understandable because of the extreme boredom induced by repetitious mythological or Biblical stories. Talented stage designers enjoyed international fame, and almost all of them were Italian. Their works were so highly admired that copper engravings were made of them. They were used as sources of inspiration by lesser designers, who decorated an almost unbelievable number of stages belonging to the petty courts of Europe and to private individuals of the noble and the wealthy bourgeois class. Certain scenes appeared again and again, standardized and often completely unrelated to the content matter of the play. The spectator would have felt cheated had there been no representation of a peasant's hut, a forest, a pompous "grande salle," a prison scene or a battlefield. And here, the ruin became important, appearing whenever the scene (and hopefully the plot!) called for the representation of terror, fear, and eeriness. From the hundreds of stage designs executed during the Baroque period, some examples should demonstrate how the ruin motif functioned in a variety of forms.

There is a great difference in the presentation of ruins before and after Ferdinando Bibiena. Ferdinando was the most important member of a family which was unique in the history of stage design. In *Varie Opere di Prospettiva* and other publications, he introduced angular perspective for the stage. This meant that it was no longer necessary to organize stage designs symmetrically, and directly facing the spectator. The audience was now drawn into the stage setting, which remained no longer merely a framed picture; stage and orchestra share three-dimensional expansion. From then on not only the Bibienas (p. 110), but all other stage designers employed Ferdinando's angular perspective. No other single step in the history of stage design had ever been of such decisive importance. Consequently the ruin grew from a mere prop into a suggestive environment which enveloped the whole scene. Needless to say, most projects for stage settings were far too imaginative to be completely adapted to the technical exigencies of the theater.

Jacques Callot

Copper engraving after Giulio Parigi's design for Second Intermezzo for the opera La Liberazione di Tirenno e d'Arnea *by Andrea Salvadori. Courtesy of the Cooper Union Museum, New York*

Giulio Parigi, the pupil of Giulio Buontalenti, and the Frenchman Jacques Callot represent the first generation of the great Flor-
entine pioneers of modern stage design with a changing set. Callot,
generally known as one of the greatest etchers, was also a very creative designer for the stage. The scene, Hell, is animated by a stun-
ning ballet of charming devils, with Lucifer himself trying very hard,
though not quite successfully, to arouse horror and fear. Obviously,
ruins of High-Renaissance buildings were considered most fitting for
this purpose by artist and audience, not because of their special
architectural form, but merely because they were ruins, provoking
terrifying associations of vengeful destruction and hopeless decay.

It is evident that in reality the symmetrical frontal view could not
be so complete and perfect as depicted in this copper engraving.
The discrepancy in scale between framing buildings and human
figures proves in itself that here, as always, the rendering is closer to
the artist's original vision than to its realization on the stage.

105

Lodovico Ottavio Burnacini

*Destroyed City. Wash Drawing. 1667. Bildarchiv der Österreichischen
Nationalbibliothek, Vienna*

Burnacini and Giacomo Torelli were the most brilliant stage designers of the early Baroque period. Burnacini was the favorite of
Emperor Leopold I of Austria, while Torelli worked for the Court
of France. Burnacini made the sets for Sbarra's opera *Il Pomo
d'Oro (The Golden Apple)* as well as for many other operas commissioned by the Imperial Court. The performance in 1667 of
Il Pomo d'Oro received international praise for the glittering splendor
of its settings and the lavish extravagance of its stage machinery.
Not only did Burnacini decorate his stage with crystal columns and
golden statues, but he also introduced the horse ballet and fireworks.
For this performance he built a special opera house holding five
thousand persons, in Vienna.

It is astonishing that Burnacini could create works so different
from the elegance and luxury of the operatic stage. Here is a scene
of macabre desolation paradoxically rendered in the traditional discipline of the pre-Bibiena stage. Burnacini has made the
architectural details so real that we forget about the inherent symbolic character of ruins, and accept them at face value as images of
the harshness of reality. We see the strong influence of tradition in
stage design in the fan-like spreading of the three streets in the background, which was the basic scheme used by Palladio for settings in
the Teatro Olimpico in Vicenza nearly one hundred years earlier.

Carlo Antonio Buffagnotti

*The Tomb of Achilles Amidst Ruins: A Stage Scene. Collection of
Donald Oenslager, New York*

Even before Ferdinando Bibiena had published his *Varie Opere di Prospettiva* in 1708 (p. 110), stage designers were breaking away from the dogma of the strictly symmetrical setting. Burnacini still adhered to this dogma—(p. 106). Nevertheless, they still composed their settings in layers which were arranged parallel to the spectator. To suggest depth was not yet a matter of great concern to them. The architectural form of this ruin, and the design of the sarcophagus are definitely Roman, in spite of the Homeric subject. Buffagnotti's concept was closer to that of the seventeenth century, especially to Poussin (p. 50) than to contemporaneous stage settings. The function of his ruins was merely to provide decorative background and not to create a mood.

Giuseppe Galli Bibiena

A Funeral Hall in the Ruins of the Colosseum.   Wash Drawing.
Collection of Donald Oenslager, New York

Giuseppe, a second-generation Bibiena, was the most prolific and inventive member of that talented family. From his earliest years, under the guidance of his father Ferdinando, he worked as a "theatrical engineer" in Dresden, Vienna, Prague, Venice, and other European cities, where he also created decorations for carnivals, funerals, and other public events. But Giuseppe was much more than a decorator: he introduced angular perspective in stage design, as this drawing clearly shows. Paradoxically, he designed and executed many catafalques at the same time that he was working on opera sets.

We also see the results of that. Without altering their basic appearance, he has transformed the tremendous vaults of the Colosseum into a funeral hall; adding monumental sarcophagi. The ruin has become a functioning structure again. Without other frills, the outlines of the vaults are accentuated by fluctuations of lights and shadow, dramatizing the original architectural forms. There are no poetic invasions of Nature; only the presence of the noble Roman past. Giuseppe painted, drew, and designed in the "grand manner," but his style was always controlled by basic rules of spacing and proportion, and he never allowed himself to indulge in theatrical effects for their own sake. Although it seems rather odd to us today, an erudite man or woman of the eighteenth century would consider it quite natural that the Colosseum should appear as a funeral hall.

Francesco Chiarottini

*Stage Setting: Interior of a Ruined Circular Temple. Ink and Wash
Drawing. 1780. Courtesy of the Cooper Union Museum, New York*

By the second half of the eighteenth century most stage designers and theatrical engineers had accepted Bibiena's technique of angular perspective. Besides the Bibienas, Quaglio and the Galliari were two of the best-known contemporary families of professional stage designers; the latter working primarily for Frederick the Great of Prussia. These families were typical in their adherence to Bibiena's methods, but at the same time they added baroque-rococo fantasies of their own. About the end of the eighteenth century, when Classicism had become the dominant form, these imaginative elements disappeared gradually.

A comparison of this drawing with Bibiena's "Funeral Hall" (p. 110) shows clearly a radical divergence in style. Both artists utilize almost identical pieces of Roman architecture—vaults and columns—but they deploy them quite differently. Bibiena's Colosseum is the work of a man who strives primarily for aesthetic effect, while Chiarottini seeks sober restraint, clarity, and structural simplicity. Chiarottini was influenced by Piranesi; especially by the etchings in *Prima Parte di Architettura e Prospettiva*. This drawing was intended for the Argentina theater in Rome, a stage for which most of the important Italian designers of the eighteenth century worked at one time or another.

Emanuele Alderani

*Stage Sets: Gothic Ruins. Ink and Wash Drawing. Courtesy of the
Cooper Union Museum, New York*

This drawing was selected not for its artistic merit, but because it illustrates a typically nineteenth-century approach to the ruin. Alderani worked for Italian, Austrian, and German theaters. Like many of his colleagues he popularized the idiom of the late eighteenth-century masters, by combining all of the traditional conceptions of ruins into one image. The result is romantic eclecticism: heterogeneous, disorganized, and facile. There is much that is odd and picturesque, but there is no inner cohesion of structure or mood. The subject of this drawing is Gothic, but Alderani also toyed with classical forms.

By contrast, Alderani's contemporary, the German architect, painter, and stage designer Karl Friedrich Schinkel pushed neo-classical design to its highest point. He created many stage settings, among which were the famous decorations for Mozart's *Zauber-flöte*. Unlike Alderani, he rejected the aesthetic values of the eighteenth century. He rarely used angular perspective, and usually built his sets in strictly symmetrical patterns. In his choice of subject material Schinkel was a forerunner of nineteenth-century eclecticism. He used Egyptian, classical, medieval, renaissance, and classical forms according to the period of history which he wished to depict. In comparison, the works of most of Schinkel's neo-classicist and romantic contemporaries seem crude and unimaginative.

CLASSICISM IN
ITALY AND FRANCE

Classicism in Italy and France

The roots of Classicism are found in the late sixteenth and early seventeenth centuries in the paintings of Poussin and the architecture of Palladio. In the seventeenth century the development of this form followed a line parallel to that of the dramatic Baroque of Bernini and Borromini. Both forms, as different as they are, were ultimately based upon the architectural heritage of Roman antiquity. Classicism, adhering to a grammar essentially dictated by Palladio, stressed a strictly formal, sometimes even mathematically rigid order, whereas Baroque was the opposite; ornate and full of exuberant emotionalism. And it was only natural that the image of ruins should reflect these stylistic divergencies.

During the seventeenth and eighteenth centuries "ruins," with few exceptions, meant Roman ruins, and this preoccupation with Rome increased as the eighteenth century progressed. Giovanni Pannini, the best-known Italian painter of ruins then, displayed encyclopedia-like "marvels of Rome"; the Colosseum, Trajan's Column, the Pyramid of Cestius, etc., in a manner which made each monument easily identifiable. Yet he completely ignored their topographical relationships, and never permitted the individual figures or groups to be anything more than incidental to the major theme: ruins. He and his followers either named their works after the main structures depicted, or simply called them "Rovine Romane" ("Roman Ruins") or some equally neutral title. Thus, unlike most of his contemporaries, who entitled their works according to rather irrelevant foreground scenes, Pannini and his followers made it very plain that the subject of their paintings was ruins, and not any human activity.

In the eighteenth century, the affinity between ruins and stage setting is especially evident in the oeuvre of G. B. Piranesi, the Venetian-born archeologist, engraver, decorator, and designer who became thoroughly Romanized in his art, and who sold his "Roman Antiquities and Views of Rome" as souvenirs to tourists. His "Prisons" and "Caprices," works of free invention, were even more dramatic, yet not intended as stage settings; architectural, without being projects for the construction of any building. Piranesi knew the stage designs of the Bibienas, but he never designed the setting for a specific play. Nevertheless, the aesthetic concept of the theater in its totality affected his works as strongly as his careful study of archeology. Unlike Pannini, Piranesi strove for accuracy in the depiction of architectural details and the locations of the monuments, while subordinating these informative aspects to emotional intensity, heightened by dramatic contrasts of light and shadow.

The French artist Hubert Robert is the third of the three foremost eighteenth-century painters of ruins. Although a generation younger than Pannini, he was closer to him than to the more visionary Piranesi. Although they differ greatly in content matter, the influence of his friend and travel companion Fragonard manifests itself in the oeuvre of Robert by the presence of a certain blitheness; a rare union of the charm of Rococo and the cooler, somewhat strict regularity of Classicism wholly absent in both Pannini and Piranesi. It is also a tribute to Robert's genius that he is able to combine visual immediacy with effects of space and depth.

By the last third of the eighteenth century, Rococo was a dying style, merely remaining the plaything of a few dilettantes. And the Classicism which had begun as a reaction against the ornateness and hedonism of Baroque had also deteriorated into a rather domesticated form which became generally known as Neoclassicism. As more and more ancient monuments were excavated and reproduced on copper engravings, the styles used in the application of classical forms to contemporary works of art underwent changes. In England, where seventeenth and eighteenth-century architects had been strongly influenced by Palladianism, Neoclassicism was not considered basically new. This was especially true since Neoclassicism differed from Palladianism more in proportions and relationships between space and volume than in architectural vernacular.

Drawings contained in archeological books such as Stuart and Revetts' *Antiquities of Athens* (1762), and Robert Adam's *Ruins of the Emperor Diocletian* (1764) were carefully studied by architects designing artificial ruins. These drawings were originally intended for use in archeological research, but they became equally important in the realms of architecture and interior decoration.

The conscious revolt against High Baroque and Rococo had begun in France with the Enlightenment and quickly spread throughout Europe. Its philosophical sanctions were supplied by the *Encyclopédie Française* (1751-1776), which contained the writings of champions of "reason and moral responsibility" such as Diderot, Alembert, and Voltaire. The English equivalent, the *Encyclopaedia Britannica,* appeared between 1768 and 1771. For aesthetic theories, the Neoclassicists drew on French, English, and German archeological texts, especially those of Johann Joachim Winckelmann. These books changed the course of development of English and French architecture, whereas in Germany their impact was more intellectual. As early as 1719, Bernard de Montaucon had published his *Antiquité Expliquée,* a book which foreshadowed systematic archeology. In 1730, the Earl of Burlington brought out a volume of Palladio's

120

manuscript drawings of Roman baths, and Piranesi (p. 128) had begun to issue his engraved series *Antichità Romane* and *Varie Vedute,* followed by *Magnificenza di Roma* in 1754. Piranesi was almost more widely read and appreciated in England than in his homeland.

Excavations had begun in Herculaneum in 1738 and in Pompeii in 1748. Findings from these cities were described by Cochin and Bellicard in 1754, and officially catalogued by the Accademia Ercolanese shortly thereafter. Le Comte de Caylus' *Recueil d'Antiquités* appeared in six volumes from 1752 to 1755, and helped to contribute to the new discipline of archeology. And Robert Wood's *Ruins of Balbec* and *Ruins of Palmyra* appeared in 1753 and 1757 respectively. Gifted scholars such as these provided authoritative justification for those who wished to believe in the perfection of antique forms.

For two generations Neoclassicism enjoyed universal acclaim, fortified by the French Revolution, with its worship of "Reason," and by Napoleon's attempt to emulate the glories of the Roman Empire. The current of Romanticism was driven underground during this period dominated by archeology, but it welled up again at the end of the Napoleonic Era.

Giovanni Paolo Pannini

Pantheon and other Monuments of Ancient Rome. Houston, Texas.
Houston Museum of Fine Arts. Courtesy, National Gallery of Art,
Washington, D.C. Kress Collection

(PLEASE REFER TO PAGE 124)

Giovanni Paolo Pannini

Rovine Romane. Collection of M. Guidi, Florence

(PLEASE REFER TO PAGE 125)

Giovanni Paolo Pannini

The juxtaposition of these two Pannini compositions shows us his ability to produce a wide range of imaginative mutations. He playfully and arbitrarily shifts, for instance, the positions of the Pantheon, the Column of Trajan, the Temple of Sibylla at Tivoli, and the equestrian statue of Marcus Aurelius. Here, the columns of the temple on the right—so prominent in the canvas opposite have disappeared, and an obelisk and a bridge are added. The "Hercules Farnese" takes the place of the sculpture of the "Nile," in the other painting. The same monuments turn up again in other canvases, together with the Pyramid of Cestius, the Colosseum, or with pieces of sculpture, like the "Dying Gaul": the insignificant in juxtaposition with the significant. Pannini likes to insert tiny human figures which are engaged in activities having no connection with the theme of the painting. He also intersperses his canvas with broken pieces of sculpture and architecture—fragments which are always radiantly evocative of the Roman past.

Giovanni Paolo Pannini

Pannini's work is rather strongly determined by commercial considerations: it was a time when, before the invention of photography, etchings and paintings were the only means for Roman tourists to keep their visual memories alive. For their benefit the familiar monuments appear, catalogue-like, in different combinations, and in complete disregard of topography. The Column of Trajan, the Pantheon, columns of the Temple of Castor, the equestrian statue of Marcus Aurelius, and triumphal arches are placed side by side. The artist's intention, of course, was to fill the canvas with as many famous sights as possible, and to reproduce them as accurately as possible, independent of their degree of decay. Today's tourist can buy similar vistas in the form of mass-produced cheap tapestries, and as in Pannini's time he may choose from many combinations of architectural highlights.

Johann H. W. Tischbein

Goethe in the Campagna, 1788. Städelsches Kunstinstitut, Frankfurt/M

This artistically rather mediocre painting, complete with ruins and reliefs, has been selected because it shows, with the clarity and irrefutability of a textbook illustration, the vacillation in aesthetic taste of the European (particularly the German) public. The work represents a watershed in the history of ideas: the definitive triumph of Classicism over the romanticizing tendencies of Baroque.

First reproduced in copper or wood engravings, later in lithographs, and still later by photographic methods, Tischbein's painting corresponds so well to the German's image of Goethe that, together with Raphael's "Sistine Madonna" it has continued to be the most popular painting in Germany since the last decade of the eighteenth century. It could be found in almost every home of the erudite ("bildungsbeflissene") German middle class. Since as painting it is aesthetically so indifferent and even shows elemental flaws in its craftsmanship, we must assume it was the subject matter which gave it such a widespread appeal.

Goethe met Tischbein in Rome, and although there were better painters in the circle of his Roman friends—Philipp Hackert for example—the great poet chose Tischbein to be his travel companion on a journey to Naples. The painter has portrayed him in an elegant, very dignified pose, seated upon some ancient fragments. An antique relief and a partially destroyed capital are beside him; the landscape, behind, interspersed with ruins, represents a mere stage backdrop.

It is interesting that it was Goethe himself—the author of *Werther's Leiden (The Sorrows of Werther),* the most famous of "Sturm und Drang" ("storm and stress") novels, and the enthusiast of Gothic architecture in his glorification of Strasbourg Cathedral—who requested that he be portrayed in this classical ambiance. The reason was that he was then under the influence of Winckelmann's *Geschichte der Kunst des Alterthums (History of the Art of Antiquity)*—since 1764 the basic text on archeology—and of Piranesi's etchings which explored and attempted to revive the Greek and Roman past.

Goethe had become one of the leading pioneers of what he termed the "classical": "The classical I would call healthy; the romantic the sick." His influence on the intellectual and cultural life of Europe was immense, and his veneration for classical ruins influenced all of the arts.

Giovanni Battista Piranesi

Roman Forum Seen from the East with the Temple of Castor and Pollux. Engraving from Views of Rome, *Plate XXXVI. The Metropolitan Museum of Art, Rogers Fund, 1941*

Piranesi—architect, painter, and restorer—was the most popular of the many eighteenth-century artists devoted to the portrayal of Roman ruins. He sold his works to scholars, collectors, antiquarians, and tourists. Besides his ability to transmit his unique, perceptive empathy with the world of antiquity, he achieved this popularity through sheer production: thirteen hundred engravings in thirty-five years. His prints stimulated Horace Walpole to speculate about the appearance of buildings such as St. James's Palace, after thousands of years.

Piranesi's genius was not limited to the interpretation of ruins. He created fantastic, bizarre prison interiors ("carceri"), strange, feverish spatial fantasies, and views of non-existent bridges, aqueducts, and tombs. His finest achievements are not in architecture, but in the graphic arts. Handling the burin and etching needle with exquisite skill, he created with the aid of these tools archeologically accurate representations of existing architecture. There is life and poetry in these drawings in addition to their meticulous craftsmanship and imaginative depictions, for he inserts trees and plants, grazing cattle, little "human interest" scenes, and country idylls.

Scholars, in recent publications, have analyzed the stylistic changes in Piranesi's oeuvre, and have pointed out that he gradually moved from a romanticizing baroque to a more classicist approach, but somehow remained one generation behind the true Neoclassicists.

Even when Piranesi tries to give objective reports of his visual experience, the emotions and personal involvement of the romantic appear, as he tries to seize and depict the unique, most significant, most dramatic element in the scene: the core of its meaning. Sometimes the dance of light and shadow; sometimes the modulation of a line, or the mere contrast of heavy masses serve him best. His technique is much too rich and diversified to be pressed into dogmatic definitions.

After his death, many artists including his children Francesco and Laura tried to carry on his work, but the result was mechanical imitation.

Piranesi's most important publications dealing with ruins are: *Le Antichità Romane, Della Magnificenza ed Architettura dei Romani,* and *Vedute di Roma*, from which this view of the Forum is taken.

Giovanni Battista Piranesi

Hadrian's Villa. Large Baths Frigidarium. Engraving from Views
of Rome, *Plate XLVI. The Metropolitan Museum of Art,
Rogers Fund, 1941*

(PLEASE REFER TO PAGE 132)

Vincenzo Scamozzi

Vaulted Passage. From Discorsi Sopra le Antichità. *1582. (Edition of 1589). Photo Courtesy of the Cooper Union Museum, New York*

(PLEASE REFER TO PAGE 133)

Giovanni Battista Piranesi

Here, Piranesi shows both his ardent interest in basic spatial effects and his acute awareness of the forces of disintegration which transform the appearance of monumental architecture. Because of his fascination with the problem of space, as well as the very fact that he lived and worked in Rome, he was attracted by the massiveness of Roman ruins rather than by the reticent nobility of classical Greek forms. When this engraving was made, the fashion was to admire Greek rather than Roman architecture, especially since Winckelmann had glorified Greek art as the irreproachable ideal.

Vincenzo Scamozzi

This print, which shows a pronounced interest in spatial effects, anticipates Piranesi's vaulted interiors, which appeared about two hundred years later. The breaks and holes in the walls and vaults do not destroy our impression of seeing a piece of architecture which once was a completely closed inner space. Nor do perspective mistakes like the distorted curve of the left wall affect our perception of the spatial image. Here, in contrast to most of Scamozzi's work, topographical details and archeological interest are irrelevant; they are subordinated to aesthetic values. Scamozzi stresses light and shadow; erosion and decay more than his contemporaries. Stone, brick, and mortar blend with the natural growth of trees and plants, and these picturesque components form an image which evokes a vague, elusive mood. Space has become topical. This was not uncommon in painting then, but was very rare in illustrations for books on architecture.

Temple of Sibylla, Tivoli

Ca. 100 B.C. Photograph Fototeca Unione, Rome

(PLEASE REFER TO PAGE 136)

Giovanni Battista Piranesi

Temple of Sibylla. Engraving. From Views of Rome, *Plate XLV.*
The Metropolitan Museum of Art, Rogers Fund, 1941

(PLEASE REFER TO PAGE 137)

135

Temple of Sibylla, Tivoli

The comparison of a painting or sketch of an ancient ruin with a modern photograph of the same subject sometimes gives us a clear concept of the imaginative and creative power of an artist. This photograph should be examined in conjunction with Piranesi's etching and Dietrich's wash drawing. We are able to appreciate the magical force of human individuality which transforms; yet leaves its subject unchanged.

Giovanni Battista Piranesi

This almost documentary record of ancient remains integrated into their natural surroundings gives us a most vivid impression of its appearance in the eighteenth century. The so-called Temple of Sibylla at Tivoli was the most popular ruin in the eighteenth century. It had been painted before by Poussin, Claude Lorrain, Salvator Rosa, and many others. It was praised in letters, poems, and essays as far back as the sixteenth century and appeared again in the form of artificial ruins in the parks and gardens of English, French, and German aristocrats as a kind of ornamental accent. The visionary force of Piranesi's imagination is even more evident if we compare this etching with the modest, charming drawing of the same subject by the German Dietrich.

Christian Wilhelm Ernst Dietrich

Temple of Sibylla, Tivoli. Wash Drawing. 1743. Staatliche Kunst-sammlungen Kupferstich-Kabinett, Dresden

(PLEASE REFER TO PAGE 140)

Pastoral Scene: Wallpaper

After an Eighteenth-century Original. 1966.
F. Schumacher & Co., New York

(PLEASE REFER TO PAGE 141)

139

Christian Wilhelm Ernst Dietrich

This sketch is typical of the innumerable drawings done by German, English, and French artists who visited Italy in the eighteenth century. The modest, reticent representation by the official painter to the Court of Saxony and Director of the Art Academy there, shows the spell of an ancient ruin in its original setting upon northern man. The work represents a charming combination of poetry and visual experience.

Pastoral Scene: Wallpaper

The eighteenth century witnessed a mania for ruins which also reached the applied arts. Ruins appeared on fabrics, especially toile de Jouy (p. 96), on chintz, as decoration on chinaware (p. 90), and as background on porcelain works (p. 92). They were used in the design of the crèche (p. 98). These are only a few examples.

Wallpaper was introduced at the end of the seventeenth century as a cheaper substitute for woven tapestries, embroidered silk, and embossed leather. The ruins on these wallpapers were of course merely decorative. No emotional response was intended or expected, even when a well-known ancient temple such as Tivoli was depicted. The ruin was part of a civilized, genteel landscape, and was often surrounded by bucolic idylls appropriately called pastorales.

J. F. Blondel

Plate CIV from Livre Nouveau ou Règles des Cinq Ordres d'Architecture par Jacques Barozzio de Vignole. *Paris. 1767. Engraved by Charpentier after Piranesi. Courtesy of the Cooper Union Museum, New York*

Blondel's whimsical additions to the strictly delineated original designs of Vignola are extremely amusing in this plate. Here, there is nothing to be learned about architectural form; nor is there emotional richness or moral instruction. The French-dominated spirit of the eighteenth century, with its desire to charm at all costs, is so strong that even the skeleton (gracefully reclining!) fails to evoke macabre reflections and we are left with a rather mundane still life.

J. F. Blondel

Plate X of Livre Nouveau ou Règles des Cinq Ordres d'Architecture par Jacques Barozzio de Vignole. *Paris. 1767. Engraved by Charpentier after C. N. Cochin. Courtesy of the Cooper Union Museum, New York*

This ruin—so different from all of the earlier, traditional renderings in sketches, engravings, and paintings—surprises us by bearing on its title page the name of Vignola: the most austere and academic of Renaissance theoreticians. Vignola's *Regola delle Cinque Ordini d'Architettura* (1562) and Serlio's treatise were carefully studied and highly respected by architects and laymen. Both works went through numerous editions and translations during the nineteenth century.

Blondel, who was court architect to Louis XV, believed deeply and honestly in Renaissance theory. But he surrendered to fashion, and tried to adapt Vignola's drawing to mid-eighteenth century taste. It is amusing to study Blondel's rather droll, typically eighteenth-century modifications and embellishments of what was originally a perfect balance of the arts of architecture, engraving, and book production. There is a grotesque dichotomy between Vignola's stern, accurate measurements, and the complacent, frilly, outspokenly rococo decorations. This dichotomy is manifest in the charming genre family scene, differing so much from the style of Vignola's columns, and in the vignette at the bottom, with its prettified ancient ruins. The work as a whole shows the high degree of period-bound subjectivism which affected the perception and graphic description of ruins in the eighteenth century.

Hubert Robert

Arch of Janus Quadrifons. Watercolor. 1781

This is one of the nine great watercolors which Robert exhibited in the Salon of 1781. He makes no attempt to achieve archeological accuracy, and we see monuments whose outlines have been softened by the addition of exuberantly growing plants and vines. There is a Laocoon group (even more baroque than the original), a sarcophagus, and stone slabs bearing inscriptions—including the name of the artist. The scene is filled with the scintillating light of the Mediterranean sun. The gracefulness of the expiring Rococo blends with the severity of neo-classical forms. In some ways this painting resembles the Memorial to Admiral Shovell executed by the Riccis about half a century earlier (p. 70). But the Riccis' work is only a facile, overly ornamented panegyric to an important man, and lacks the visual sincerity of Robert's painting.

Hubert Robert

*Arches in Ruins. The Metropolitan Museum of Art.
Gift of J. Pierpont Morgan, 1917*

"Robert des Ruines" was outstanding among the eighteenth-century French painters who specialized in this macabre motif. He was a greater painter than Pannini, who seems pedantic in comparison, and who lacked Robert's subtle feeling for the unique aesthetic qualities of decay. As Piranesi was master of this subject matter in the graphic arts, so was Robert in painting.

The French painter Fragonard and Robert were good friends, and had studied together in Italy for eleven years. Fragonard, however, saw ruins from a different viewpoint, and was not interested in using them as major motifs in his paintings. But Robert stresses the same spatial values which we find in Piranesi's works, and in spite of the differences in their techniques—painting vs. etching—there is a similarity in their response to nuances of emotion, mood, and atmosphere, which are presented gently yet persuasively. Robert likes to combine real and imaginary ruins, and to embed them in a picturesque landscape. The human figures are used primarily to establish standards for measuring proportion. Besides oil paintings and wash drawings, Robert created decorative panels and designed artificial ruins for royal parks such as Versailles and Marly.

Hubert Robert

Colonnade and Canal. Wash Drawing. Montpellier, France

In this preparatory sketch, Robert was concerned with the two main problems of his art: clarification of spatial relationships and differentiation of tonal values. The drawing looks like an improvisation, which it decidedly is not. It appears vague and romantic only because it is uncompleted. The influence of his friend Fragonard on his brush stroke is more evident here than in most of his completed works.

Hubert Robert

*The Great Gallery of the Louvre. 1796. Formerly at Tsarskoje-Tselo,
Russia*

(PLEASE REFER TO PAGE 154)

Hubert Robert

Ruins of the Great Gallery of the Louvre. 1796. Formerly at Tsarskoje-Tselo, Russia

(PLEASE REFER TO PAGE 155)

Hubert Robert

Robert was appointed Garde du Musée du Roi—Administrator of the Galeries of the Louvre—in 1784 by a decree of Louis XVI. Surviving the Revolution, he regained his post under Napoleon. This painting, showing Robert's project for the remodelling of the Great Gallery by the addition of skylights, was submitted to the Salon of 1796. Like all of his work it shows his tendency to indulge in grand perspectives. Many of the paintings which appear in this scene—Raphael's "Holy Family" for example—are still among the treasures of the Louvre.

Hubert Robert

Robert's painting of the gallery of the Louvre pulsates with human activity. Here is the same interior, fallen into decay; weathered and tinted by age. But it has not lost its grand style and some architectural details even remain. The solitude and silence are relieved only by the presence of a few artists, who are copying famous pieces of sculpture such as the "Apollo Belvedere" and the remains of one of Michelangelo's "Slaves," which lie scattered in the foreground. Robert's ruin-studded fantasy is a vision of the fate which awaits both the objects he loved so well, and the architecture which houses them.

Joseph Gandy

The Bank of England in Ruins. Watercolor. Soane Museum, London. Photo from The Life and Works of Sir John Soane

Artists such as Gandy, imitating Hubert Robert's vision of the melancholy fate of the Louvre (p. 153), liked to paint churches, public buildings, and monuments as they might appear in an advanced state of decay. Gandy was a minor architect, a pupil of Sir John Soane, who designed the Bank of England. This watercolor is inferior to Robert's fantasy, but nevertheless the artist succeeds in creating an impressive blend of stones and plant life. Gandy, like Robert, concentrated on the interpretation of space. The accent on the picturesque qualities of the scene betrays the long shadow of Piranesi, who also influenced Cuitt's etchings of English cathedrals (p. 171). It is ironic that the Bank of England, a masterpiece of the purest English neo-classical style, should be chosen to represent such an ambiguous motif.

Gothic
Romanticism in
England and Germany

Gothic Romanticism in England and Germany

The short introductory remarks to each section must be expanded when dealing with the eighteenth century, for it was then that the general interest in ruins was most intense, and the motif reached its peak both in landscaping and in the applied arts. Innumerable artificial ruins appeared in parks, and even the most everyday household utensils were decorated with images of decayed buildings and monuments. The oil paintings, watercolors, woodcuts, copper engravings, and etchings which have been selected for this chapter have one thing in common—they are representative of the way in which the awareness and response to the visual, tangible results of the ravages of time underwent radical aesthetic and philosophical transformations beginning in the early eighteenth century. In many instances these changes were the direct results of stimulation by works of poetry, fiction, and especially scholarly publications.

Considering the fact that French and Italian artists of the century almost always chose real or imaginary classical remainders as subject matter, there is a surprisingly rich variety of interpretations in their works. During the first third of the century we rarely find depictions of ruined medieval churches or monasteries, for in France and Italy these "Gothic" constructions were considered barbarous and uncouth; vestiges of an architecturally degraded age in which builders were apostates from the only real civilization—that of the ancient Mediterranean world.

But in the North, removed from the scenes of antiquity, consciousness of the past was synonymous with the medieval relics which were scorned by the Latins. There, contemporary philosophy and literature, especially the writings of Jean Jacques Rousseau, Horace Walpole, and the German "Sturm und Drang" ("storm and stress") group of the second half of the century contributed to a resurgence of interest in the Middle Ages. These writers were unanimous in their praise of "Gothic" architecture as being closer to nature than any style based on antiquity. At the beginning of the eighteenth century, however, when the artificial-ruin fad was in its infancy, the preference was still for classical forms, and the first sham ruins were "antiquish."

161

In literature, as well as in architecture, the English have always sought a closer association with nature than the continental Europeans. And in the eighteenth century, if an English gentleman wished to build a lodge, a "temple of friendship," a cowshed, a dairy, or even a storage place for garden utensils, he chose a style which would fuse itself intimately with the surroundings and which would not be felt as an obtrusion among his beloved trees, bushes, lawns, and plants. Rejecting the French formal garden of Le Nôtre, these gentry wanted the imaginary landscapes of painters such as Salvator Rosa, Poussin, and Ruisdael translated into reality.

Ruins by their "otherness" soon came to be the metaphorical vehicles for the thoughts and feelings of the cultured Englishman of every social class, and a source of inspiration for many writers of varying degrees of talent. Indeed, one may state that then, literature owed more to visual art than visual art to literature. Joseph Addison and Alexander Pope loved Gothic forms and the more picturesque aspects of nature. Later in the century Thomas Warton and the great poet Thomas Gray, whom Walpole considered the most important literary figure of the Gothic Revival, gave further impetus to the passion for artificial ruins. Walpole, who from 1747-1753 transformed Strawberry Hill into a Gothic structure complete with turrets, pinnacles, and spires, was the first to put the theories of the Gothic Revival into practice. However, he also had a deep appreciation for the beauties of Roman ruins, which he saw in 1740. He was enchanted by the Temple of Sibylla (p. 134) and wrote enthusiastically about the subterranean ruins of Herculaneum, "from which the scholars could learn so much." And yet Walpole never built an artificial ruin at Strawberry Hill.

"Artificial ruins must be seen to be disbelieved," quipped a thoroughly convinced rationalist. This witty yet terribly banal aphorism summarizes the attitude of modern man toward this art form. On the other hand, it is true that the romantic yearning for broken columns, dilapidated arches, and half-ruined bridges and grottoes was in many instances merely emotional self-indulgence; a trifling flirtation with melancholy feelings which would eventually make the "landscape of fantasy degenerate into the picturesque." (Sir Kenneth Clark)

The deification of the French and Italian masters of the seventeenth century, the re-discovery of the eerie charm of Gothic architecture, and contemporary literature, with its abundant descriptions of ruins—these were the influences which raised a vague, generalized, sentimental interest in ruins to the level of a connoisseurship best exemplified by the Society of Dilettanti. England had (and still has) many medieval ruins, but obviously not enough to satisfy the eighteenth-century landed gentry. Their motto seems to have been "to each his own ruin," and in spite of bitter quarrels over the subject, it didn't much matter whether the building were Gothic or classical. Henry Home asked in *Elements of Criticism*: "Should a ruin be of Gothic or of Greek form? The first, I think, since it shows the triumph of time over strength, a melancholic though not unpleasant thought; a Greek ruin lets you rather divine the triumph of Barbarianism over taste, a sad and discouraging thought."

This entire development would have been impossible without radical changes in landscape design; the creation of a new concept of the natural environment. By the end of the eighteenth century practically every petty nobleman in Europe had in his park—within his means and more often beyond—what he liked to think of as a replica of the glories of Versailles. In any case, the Gothic Revival in architecture meant a revolution in taste; a liberation from formal restrictions in favor of the imaginative and picturesque.

Tintern Abbey, Monmouthshire

British Travel Association Photograph

Tintern Abbey has always been immensely popular as the ideal of a monastic ruin for both tourists and artists. Lord Walter Fitz Richard founded it in 1131 as a Cistercian house, and it was enlarged during the thirteenth century. The church proper was built between 1270 and 1320, with some later additions. After the catastrophe of the secularization in 1534, it was inhabited by vagabonds, and masons used it for a quarry. Later generations were deterred from destroying the building by its sheer strength of construction, and were also probably overwhelmed by its austere dignity. Thus most of the damage was brought about by natural forces; by corrosion, since rain, wind, and snow attacked an interior unprotected by a roof.

In the eighteenth century the Duke of Beaufort attempted to preserve the remainders and "clean" Tintern Abbey—an unusual undertaking in that century. Fortunately, he did not do too much damage. Although the exterior is less impressive than the interior, it still conveys the architectural concepts of space and volume better than any other Gothic ruin. Nature and architecture interweave miraculously to create the image of a legendary past so dear to the British people.

Tintern Abbey

*Nave, Looking West. Photo from M. R. James and A. H. Thompson.
Abbeys. London. 1926*

(PLEASE REFER TO PAGE 168)

J. M. Turner

Tintern Abbey. Watercolor. Victoria and Albert Museum,
Crown Copyright

(PLEASE REFER TO PAGE 169)

Tintern Abbey

For centuries—in fact until the end of the nineteen hundreds—
the interior of Tintern Abbey appeared as it does in this view of
the nave, looking west, though perhaps during the Middle Ages it
was less overgrown with ivy and other foliage. Details of pointed
arches, pillars, the delicate tracery of the window—all examples of
Gothic workmanship—are so well preserved that they provide material for academic studies: the last and most pathetic catastrophe to
befall a symbol of medieval dedication to God. The rhythmical sequence of the original bays and the relationship between nave and
transepts can still be felt and can easily be pictured in our imagination. But the grammar of motifs is not the decisive reason for the
widespread reverence aroused by these ruins. Tintern Abbey was,
and continues to be venerated because of the powerful evocative
force of its spatial relationships, which draw the onlooker into the
past, and allow him to imagine the building as it once stood unim-
paired.

J. M. Turner

Turner painted his impression of Tintern Abbey from almost the same angle of vision as the 1926 photograph (p. 166). Compared with most of the oeuvre of this fanatical colorist, who blurred the outlines of his forms with veils of incandescent light, this watercolor appears almost realistic. But in fact, Turner has as usual dramatized what he saw, and thus remains true to his manner of using light as a romanticizing force. A comparison with the photo shows the high degree of the artist's subjectivism. His approach is best described by Archdeacon Coxe, writing in 1801, and still reflecting eighteenth-century attitudes: "Nature has added her ornaments to the decoration of art; some of the windows are wholly obscured, others partially shaded with tufts of ivy, or edged with lighter foliage; the tendrils creep along the walls, wind round the pillars, wreath the capitals, or hanging down in clusters obscure the space beneath. . . . "Ornamental fragments of the roof, remains of cornices and columns, rich pieces of sculpture, sepulchral stones, and mutilated figures of monks and heroes, whose ashes repose within these walls, are scattered on the greensward, and contrast present desolation with former splendour." (M. R. James and A. H. Thompson. *Abbeys.* London, 1926)

Fountains Abbey, Yorkshire

Chapel of the Nine Altars. British Travel Association Photograph

(PLEASE REFER TO PAGE 172)

Fountains Abbey

The Tower and Nave. Etching by George Cuitt the Younger

(PLEASE REFER TO PAGE 173)

171

Fountains Abbey, Yorkshire

This abbey, like Tintern Abbey, was founded in the twelfth century by Cistercians, and shares similar characteristics. The choir, the
eastern transept, and the Chapel of the Nine Altars were executed
during the first part of the thirteenth century; the big window and the
tower not until the end of the fifteenth. There is little to be said for
this photograph. It is as dry and banal as a list of dates. Nothing
whatsoever of the singular charm of this ruin—a result of the beauty
of the original, enriched even by the accidents of the process of disintegration, and its gradual fusion with nature—has been caught.
The wonderful heterogeneity of these Gothic forms, which stem from
so many periods, has been sterilized and purified by this "objective"
photograph. Fountains Abbey is an especially lovely medieval relic,
and needs the subjective rendering of an artist to breathe life into it;
to convey its bewitching mood; a mood which is reflected in literature by Gothic tales of terror and enchantment.

Fountains Abbey

The fascination of Fountains Abbey remained so strong that nineteenth-century artists continued to glorify it. Cuitt included this etching, together with historical comments, in his album *Wanderings and Pencillings Amongst Ruins of the Olden Time*. He published his book in 1848, a generation later than what is usually called the Period of Romanticism. Cuitt's infatuation with the "picturesque" was as ardent as that of any eighteenth-century painter. Here, the ruin has almost become a part of nature; commingled with the profusion of feathery trees, dense bushes, and climbing tendrils. The stones seem to corrode and crumble before our eyes. The influence of Piranesi's work—conceptually and technically—is obvious.

Dunluce Castle, County Antrim, Northern Ireland

British Travel Association Photograph

There are almost as many decayed medieval castles in Northern Ireland as in England proper. This one was built by Richard de Burgh, Earl of Ulster, about 1300, with a few later additions. The two remaining cylindrical towers allow us to recognize the original rectangular form of the overall plan. The corner of a Jacobean house built on the original foundation is barely discernible, and in no way disturbs the impression of hostile, dreary solitude with indications of human warmth. The somber masses of the castle, set in a bleak landscape, look as though they could provide the setting for some gloomy, horrible tale of northern mythology.

Dürnstein Castle, Wachau, Austria

Twelfth Century. Photo, Prof. Gustav A. Fenz, Vienna

Dürnstein Castle, another medieval ruin, owes its fame to the fact that England's King Richard the Lion-Hearted was kept prisoner there 1192-1193. The impression of its destroyed walls and towers is entirely unlike that of Dunluce Castle (p. 174), and so are our emotional reactions. Whereas the latter's decay was caused essentially by gradual erosion through the centuries, Dürnstein was destroyed during the Thirty Years' War by attacking Swedes in 1645. This difference is significant. In Dürnstein, the jagged forms of what is still left show the impact of enemy action, while in Dunluce the perpetuity of centuries has softened the symptoms of destruction. The contrast between Dürnstein's abrupt, towering forms and the soft curves of the peaceful valley of the Danube River represents persuasively the drama of man destroying what man has built.

Joseph Wright of Derby

The Old Man and Death. Ca. 1774. Courtesy Wadsworth Atheneum, Hartford, Conn.

As the eighteenth century advanced, the poetic conception of ruins as objects which should provoke gentle, sweetly melancholy reflections about the sad but inevitable decay of everything in the universe seemed to evaporate. Its place was taken by harsh images of despair and death. The quintessence of this new attitude is grotesquely illustrated in Wright's paintings. The ruin has become a symbol of the ineluctable and horrible disintegration which awaits all things: nature (the barren, twisted tree), human works (the decayed building), and man.

Wright was a very mediocre artist. He was a bizarre personality, and he always sought unusual subjects; especially ones which showed extraordinary effects of light. Thus, he painted glowing forges, the then-new factories, catastrophes involving fire, and pyrotechnics. In this confrontation of an old peasant with death, Wright is even more of an sensationalist than usual. He focuses on two gestures: the peremptory invitation of the skeleton, and the horrified, yet hopeless refusal of the old man. The obviousness of the symbolism is embarrassing; the colors are motley and inappropriate. The work shows how degraded and trite once-meaningful philosophical ideas associated with ruins had become, and how the delicate emotions of mid-century had changed into banalities.

Carl Blechen

The Burnt-out Cathedral. Oil on Paper. Staatliche Museen, Berlin

Blechen's paintings, in spite of their basically romantic mood, have an almost impressionistic immediacy. Yet, like his friend Caspar David Friedrich (p. 184), he was stimulated by Ruisdael (p. 68) and other seventeenth-century Dutch masters. On the other hand, the Italian landscape, which he had admired during his youthful travels, also made a deep impression on Blechen, to further complicate the individual style of this many-sided artist. Ruins as such were never pivotal to his work. Thus he relies upon the suffering human figure in this scene to convey the tragic mood, rather than upon the demolished building in the background.

Heisterbach Ruin

Steel Engraving. Nineteenth Century

The ruin of Heisterbach in the Rhineland is one of the most famous in Germany. There is a popular legend about it which is a counterpart of the Rip van Winkle story. A monk, returning to his abbey, was not aware that a thousand years had passed since he went away. The miracle occurred because he doubted that "a thousand years in thy sight are but as yesterday when it is past." (Psalm 90)

This Cistercian abbey was founded in 1189, and consecrated in 1227, to be partially razed in the secularization of 1803. Like Sadeler's engraving of the Nymphaeum Aquae Julia (p. 30), the apse is especially impressive by its emphasis on the dimension of depth. In both works the spatial relationships of the original remain undisturbed: they were neither concealed nor modified by the destructiveness of nature or man. The structural similarity of the Roman Nymphaeum and the medieval German abbey church refers, of course, not to the intact original buildings, but only to what remains of them in the form of ruins.

Caspar David Friedrich

*Ruins of a Monastery and Church Yard in Snow. 1819. Berlin
Nationalgalerie. Photo, Prof. Herbert von Einem, Bonn*

A contemporaneous critic called this painting "a picture of death without hope, without the eternal star of love," and that is precisely the impression the German romantic painter wanted to evoke. He and his friend Philipp Otto Runge express feelings similar to those of the English romanticists, whereas the later generation of German romantic painters like Moritz von Schwind and Carl Spitzweg always managed to tint their dramatic solemnity with a little *Gemütlichkeit*. These German artists enriched their canvases with literary allusions, just as German romantic poetry is filled with references to the visual arts. The lonely, silent procession of monks, coming from nowhere, is slowly walking, as though in a sad, heavy dream, toward the Sacrament. The snow, the terrible sense of numbing, never-ending, cosmic iciness, the sharply etched profiles of the naked trees, the battered crosses, and the ultimate symbol of death—a half-open grave—contribute to this vision of despair. The scene is dominated by the ruined apse which points toward skies which do not seem to give much promise of redemption. A comparison of mood and subject matter with Ruisdael's "The Cemetery" (p. 68) suggests itself, though the styles differ.

John Constable

Hadleigh Castle. Before 1829. Reproduced by Courtesy of Trustees of the Tate Gallery, London

This sketch, which shows no attempt to achieve verisimilitude, reflects the typical romantic approach to ruins more than any other of Constable's works. It also shows his favorite technique of fusing castles and cathedrals with the landscape. The ruin occupies the commanding position over other elements of the picture: the ground, the occasional trees, the clouds; everything is *quasi* background music to the decayed castle. A study of Constable's writings helps to explain the paradox of how this pioneer of modern landscape painting succumbed emotionally to the prevailing theories of Romanticism, whereas in technique he was two generations ahead of his time in his handling of the landscape. The difference between his preparatory sketches and his final paintings sheds further light on this problem. In the sketches he expresses his feelings without restraint, whereas he tends to adapt the paintings to the conventions of the age.

Thomas Cole

The Course of Empire: *Desolation. 1836. Courtesy of the New-York Historical Society, New York City*

Thomas Cole, born in England, was brought to America at the age of nine, and became more "American" than most contemporary native-born artists. He was the father of the "Hudson River School", the first original American school of painting. Deeply moved by the natural beauty which he saw in the Eastern States, he began to portray their woods, rivers, lakes, and tumbling waterfalls. After his first encounter with Europe as a man of twenty-eight, his approach changed—not as one would think in the direction of French or Italian landscape painting, but instead toward the German Romanticism of that time. Cole's interest was no longer in the landscape *per se*, which he had heretofore painted so well, but in its potential religious or historical meaning. And at that point, ruins began to play a decisive role in his oeuvre.

Cole believed that the best way to reveal his insights was to paint a narrative series, of which the best known is the "Course of Empire" (1836), inspired by Gibbon's *Decline and Fall of the Roman Empire*. Cole envisions the final apocalyptic stage of history— "Desolation"—as a bleak, ruin-studded landscape, emptied of the human life which is depicted in the preceding parts of the series. This agglomeration of architectural fragments in no way mirrors a destroyed townscape, as did the visions of earlier artists. In spite of the essential pragmatism of the series as a whole, this tremendous ultimate vision is highly emotional. Subtle atmospheric nuances persuasively convey virtually every romantic connotation of ruins, yet the visual qualities of the painting do not impair its illustrative merits. The work presents philosophical history in the form of a grand image.

Coventry Cathedral, Warwickshire

Photograph taken after World War II. British Travel Association

There is a striking analogy between the sixteenth-century remains of Tintern Abbey and the twentieth-century ruins of St. Michael's in Coventry, a red sandstone cathedral begun in 1133 on the foundations of a Norman church, and completed ca. 1433. Obvious similarities appear as we look toward the tracery, but more important ones are seen in the remains of the roofless naves. Both structures are framed by parts of their original walls, and the relationship between nave and aisles is still recognizable. The separating pillars and arches of Tintern Abbey are still partially intact, while only the bases of those in Coventry remain. After German warplanes had leveled St. Michael's, crowds of believers continued to gather and pray, standing under the grey English skies in the now open expanse. And who, looking at the tragic, skeletal ruin, and then at the triumphant, outspokenly modern phoenix of the twentieth-century church, could not be a believer? The hollow shell of the Gothic edifice with its windows gaping into emptiness meets the tremendous mass of the new cathedral at a ninety-degree angle: an entirely original spatial conception—crucifixion and resurrection translated into architectural terms.

ARTIFICIAL
RUINS

Artificial Ruins

The artificial ruin is inseparably connected with the new concept of landscaping: the "natural" English park. As mentioned before, both ruin and park were reactions against the formal French garden of Le Nôtre and his followers, to whom the aesthetic distinction between building and park lay not in form and function, but in material; the one being composed of stone, brick, mortar, and wood; the other of trees, bushes, hedges, and lawns, all of which were subordinated to one grand design. The geometrically organized gardens and parks which they constructed during the last part of the seventeenth and the entire eighteenth centuries were conceived as architecture formed out of the elements of nature, whereas the guiding idea of the English "reformers" was to create an environment in which the works of man and of Nature should meet as equals. The English architects animated their parks and gardens with "follies"—artificial grottoes, Chinese pagodas, half-destroyed bridges, bark huts, and waterfalls. Architects and landscape designers alike would, however, have objected to the use of the word "animated" to describe the function of their decorations, for they wanted them to be taken seriously, as objects to stimulate the deepest, most exalted emotions and somber philosphical reflections about the impermanence of human works and the ultimate triumph of Nature.

We should not think of the artificial ruin as a unique development of the eighteenth century, for its aesthetic possibilities had been seen long before that time. Vasari relates in his *Lives* that in 1510 the Duke of Urbino commissioned Girolamo Genga—architect, archeologist, stage designer, painter, and sculptor—to erect what we would call an artificial ruin in the park at Pesaro. The structure was completed and was mentioned by several writers as being a great marvel. They unfortunately neglected to describe it, but at least they provided proof that the English architects had been anticipated.

Artificial ruins—those "mighty pictures in three dimensions"—reflected the poetic images contained in eighteenth-century letters, diaries, and poems with much greater force than paintings or engravings could achieve. For these literary works were replete with accounts of decayed monasteries, dilapidated, roofless churches, caved-in vaults, graveyards, and haunted towers—a sinister, crepuscular world inhabited, together with ghosts, by Nature's less-attractive but nevertheless morbidly fascinating creatures: bats, adders, wolves, owls, etc. These props almost invariably evoked a delicious shudder of terror in the poets and writers of the period, and presumably had a similar effect on the reader. Since Rose Macaulay has brilliantly analyzed all of this in *Pleasure of Ruins*, there is no need to repeat her fine scholarship and poetic descriptions.

The first book to provide direct motivation for the construction of artificial ruins was Batty Langley's *New Principles of Gardening* (1728). But his suggestion that "these ruins may either be painted upon canvas or actually built in that manner with brick and covered with plastering in imitation of stone" is rather hard to take, even for the antiquarian (p. 200).

Observation of actual ruins and of nature was much more influential than theoretical treatises like Langley's. William Kent, though only a third-rate painter, was the first important English landscape architect—the "father of modern gardening" as Walpole called him. Like most of his contemporaries, he was influenced by Claude Lorrain, Poussin, and Salvator Rosa, all of whom appear many times in this text. He also studied the Dutch landscapists, and his works reflect reminiscences of his travels in Italy. Kent designed the park at Stowe for the Earl of Burlington, and both artist and patron shared the conviction that Nature abhors a straight line. Kent very logically planned the roads and rivulets of Stowe in accordance with this precept. He planted his boskets with careful attention to color combinations of the foliage and accents of light and shadow. But more important in our context, he provided the park with "a glut of buildings"; interspersing Chinese pagodas and classical ruins; placing artificial dead trees and fragments of tree trunks in locations which would give the maximum picturesque effect. He constructed a "Temple of Ancient Virtue" and its counterpart, a "Temple of Modern Virtue." The latter, ironically, is more emotionally evocative and artistically satisfying than its twin.

Kent's successor in this revolution in landscape design was Sir William Chambers, who enhanced Kew Gardens with pagodas, mosques, and with his famous artificial Roman arch (p. 224).

Earlier yet, in 1746 the Duke of Cumberland built a magnificent artificial ruin which he called Virginia Water (p. 206). Here he erected genuine ancient columns and augmented them with artificial parts.

The amateur architect Sanderson-Miller was the most prolific of the many contemporary builders of sham ruins. The famous Folly of Edgehill (1743) was his work, as was Hagley Park Castle (1745). Both were much admired by Walpole, with whom Sanderson-Miller carried on an interesting professional correspondence. Sanderson-Miller began his career by experimenting with Gothic forms, and ended a confirmed classicist. That nobody protested his use of perishable, shoddy materials is ample commentary on the contemporary lack of feeling for the true spirit of architecture.

There is probably no better way to acquire insight into the aesthetic climate of England in the second half of the eighteenth century than to turn to the writings of William Gilpin. Gilpin was an ardent traveller and knew the English countryside thoroughly, although he was rather dry and uninspired as a painter and graphic artist. His best-known book, *Observations on the River Wye* (1782) reflects his passionate search for "picturesque beauty"—a longing and an aesthetic ideal shared by so many Englishmen of his generation.

Germany, which had fallen behind England and France in the development of the visual arts because of her unfortunate economic and political situation, looked with great interest and envy at the splendors of Versailles. In the eighteenth century, when Germany finally experienced an architectural awakening, it took a threefold form: a new interest in both ruined and intact Gothic architecture, the erection of artificial Gothic ruins in newly landscaped parks, and the belated completion of the masterworks which had been begun in the Middle Ages, but which had remained unfinished during the troubled centuries which followed. So the protest against French formalistic rigidity found its expression in parks and palaces much later in Germany than in England. The magnificent High Gothic Cathedral at Cologne, for example, was begun in 1243. Its construction was interrupted in the fifteenth century, and it required the rather artificial stimulation of the Gothic Revival to raise enough interest (and money) to finish the job in 1880. In another region of Germany, the Marienburg, near Danzig, was also restored to its original Gothic form only in the nineteenth century.

The influence of literature was as strong in Germany as it was in England. The aesthetic climate of eighteenth-century Germany is often referred to as the "Triumph der Empfindsamkeit" ("The Triumph of Sentimentality"). It represented a typically German systematisation and an almost dogmatic standardization of the new approach to nature and landscape, and was mirrored especially in the poetry of Ewald Christian von Kleist and the Swiss Salomon Gessner. In landscaping and artificial ruins, the new style found its expression in the writings of Christian G. L. Hirschfeld, who was both professor of philosophy and landscape architect. His *Theorie der Garten Kunst* (1777-1782) was influential throughout Europe. Goethe, in *Wahlverwandtschaften,* described a park which was designed according to Hirschfeld's ideas. The uniquely German interpretation of European Romanticism reached its epitome in Wilhelm Heinrich Wackenroder's *Herzensergiessungen eines Kunstliebenden Klosterbruders* (1797). We can still see the evidence of Romanticism expressed in the style of the royal parks at Wörlitz, Weimar, Potsdam, Nymphenburg (p. 202), and Schönbrunn (p. 226). The handful of artificial ruins erected in Germany during the last decade of the eighteenth century or later were feeble and eclectic and failed to express the sentiments which in other countries brought forth so many

197

charming creations. The German "romantic" ruin—romantic in its popular, vague, and diluted connotations—was (and still is) thought of as a decayed castle, preferably on the banks of the Rhine or the Danube, whereas in England the typical romantic image is that of the secularized abbey.

Although the fad was international, no country could compare with England in enthusiasm for artificial ruins. As mentioned before, the writings of Rousseau had prepared first the French intellectuals and then the general public with a set of thoughts and feelings appropriate to the contemplation of artificial ruins.

Yet the formal, geometric style of the French garden often transformed these pieces of sham architecture into mere decorations giving an impression of frozen sentimentality. This was not the case in the English landscaped park, where Nature, relatively undisturbed, provided the proper romantic setting.

In the second part of the eighteenth century the concept of the English garden was spreading throughout Europe; relatively late in France, where the formal garden was too deeply established. Only a few artificial ruins appeared there before the middle of the century, and they never became really popular until Neoclassicism began to take root there. To mention one example: the Desert de Retz (p. 222) was a colossal, ruined Greek column designed as a "residence," a shock indeed to those who believe in functionalism.

A two-dimensional counterpart to artificial ruins may be found in the works of Charles Louis Clérisseau. Not content with executing paintings of ruins, he composed "ruin rooms" whose walls were covered with naturalistic projections of classical ruins in different stages of decay. Clérisseau's feeling for neo-classical forms was largely influenced by the fact that he travelled and worked for many years with the Adam brothers.

There is an interesting connection between the revolutionary political ideas of the end of the century and the aesthetic interpretation of ruins. For suddenly ruins were no longer charming playthings at the service of those who wished to indulge in delightful reveries. Now they must stimulate the intellect and cause the spectator to reflect about the passage of time, the meaning of history, and the destiny of man. One might say that morality was replacing charm. In Constantin François Chasseboeuf Volney's *Ruins, or Meditations on the Revolution of Empires*, published in 1791, the elevation of ruins into universal symbols of the philosophy of history is achieved with great literary power. And in *The Decline and Fall of the Roman Empire* Gibbon mentions that he received the inspiration for his life's work while contemplating the shattered remains of Imperial Rome. So ruins were now memorials of departed grandeur and of the transience and fragility of that which in appearance was indestructible; tangible warning to the living of the impermanence of stone and flesh.

During the first decades of the nineteenth century, ruins with their associations still haunted many great creative minds. Walter Scott was as "ruin conscious" as was Walpole two generations earlier. It was not until the second half of the nineteenth century that the interest in ruins disappeared, becoming submerged in the prevailing eclecticism which played with elements of virtually every period and which sacrificed historical association.

We must turn to the twentieth century for an occasional reoccurrence of the ruin theme in the visual arts. But the ruin is no longer a symbol related to an intellectually definable, teleological current of history: now it represents primarily the religious anxiety and physical and moral uncertainty with which we are all familiar.

Batty Langley

New Principles of Gardening. *Plate XIX. London. 1728*

This is one of the earliest books in which the "New Principles of Gardening" were expounded. However, a discussion of the differences between the style of French formal gardens and parks, still dictated by Le Nôtre, and the revolutionary English landscaping would be out of place here. Our interest is in the appearance of the ruin as an integral part of the new landscaping. Langley suggests that these ruins "in the old Roman manner" either be painted on canvas(!) as the prospect of an alley, or actually constructed and used as scenic background for tree-framed perspectives. The latter suggestion was one of the earliest inclusions of "ornamental" buildings in parks. Later in his career Langley's preference was for Gothic rather than Roman forms.

Magdalenenklause, Nymphenburg

Foto Inter Nationes

Magdalenenklause was built by the Bavarian court architect Joseph Effner. Like the fountains, bark huts, pavilions, and pagodas which dot the Nymphenburg Park near Munich, it is intended as a diminutive architectural decoration. The dollhouse-like buildings in this park were not designed for any function—they were erected for amusement, or in the case of Magdalenenklause, for contemplation. The size of these tiny structures contrasts with the gigantic dimensions of the Nymphenburg Palace (built 1663-1726).

Magdalenenklause was intended to be a hermitage for the aged Grand Elector Max Emmanuel—a place of refuge from court life; and its craggy, ruinous appearance supposedly symbolizes withdrawal from worldly pleasures and cares.

Its design shows the transition from the usual late Baroque or Rococo, found in many Italian and French parks, to the artificial ruin. Basically, it is made of shells, stalactites, and tuff, but there are also broken pieces of architecture. Pseudo-Gothic forms mingle with a sort of playful Baroque. Sham-brick walls, which seem to wither away, are only partially covered with stucco. There are artificial cracks to indicate decay, and within, a statue of the repentant Magdalen by Joseph Volpini. The elaborate interior decoration suggests the same fashionable emotions that are expressed in the exterior design.

Ruined Temple of Bacchus at Paineshill, Surrey

About 1750. From Osvald Sirén China and Gardens of Europe of the Eighteenth Century, *Plate XXXV*

Charles Hamilton erected a rather modest artificial ruin, sometimes erroneously called a mausoleum, in the park of Paineshill. The building was praised by Horace Walpole and by the Prince de Ligne, who was one of the few contemporary Frenchmen who took an interest in English parks and artificial ruins. Both men found it especially enchanting because of its lovely natural setting. Although originally intended to look like a ruin, the temple certainly did not look as decayed in 1750 as it does today. The columns of the façade have fallen away, causing the collapse of large parts of the pediment, which was decorated by a relief. Only the triglyphs and metopes, and a few capitals of the vanished columns evidence the classicist ambitions of the architect. The ruin is definitely more interesting to the poet than to the antiquarian or archeologist.

Virginia Water

Windsor Great Park. 1746. Photograph, Dr. Richard P. Wunder, Washington, D. C.

In his poem by that name, written in 1712, Alexander Pope had already praised Windsor Park, where this artificial ruin of unique character still attracts many visitors. Roman columns and pieces of architrave were brought to England from the ancient Roman town of Leptis Magna in Tripoli, in the mid-eighteenth century, in order to build Virginia Water. Eighteenth-century stonework was substituted for missing fragments, but fortunately no attempt was made to reconstruct an ancient temple. Replacement pieces were deliberately given a ruinous appearance. The overall view is especially impressive, since the setting is dispersed over a wide area, which lets the architecture melt gracefully into its natural surroundings, which emphasizes its ornamental effects more than its archeological interest.

Robert Adam

Design for an Artificial Ruin. Ca. 1756. Victoria and Albert
Museum, London

(PLEASE REFER TO PAGE 210)

Robert Adam

Design for an Artificial Ruin in the Park at Keddleston. Ca. 1759.
Victoria and Albert Museum, Crown Copyright

(PLEASE REFER TO PAGE 211)

Robert Adam

This elevation must be considered a preparatory sketch for Adam's project for an artificial ruin at Keddleston (p. 209). The organization of the whole is identical, and the elements which make up the left side are already present in this drawing. The rendering is offhand and casual, for the artist is mainly concerned with representing the antique decor, whereas in his cross-sectional plan he is more rigid and exacting, and brings out the three-dimensional effects through the play of light and shadow.

Robert Adam

When he went to Rome in 1755, Robert Adam joined a group of avant-garde artists centered in that city. These architects, painters, and sculptors were interested both in the Greek and Roman art rediscovered in the Renaissance, and that which had been found in newly excavated Pompeii and Herculaneum. Led by Raphael Mengs, these artists pioneered the neo-classical movement. Most of them were competent archeologists. Small wonder that the founder of modern scientific archeology, Johann Joachim Winckelmann, who was in Rome working on his *Geschichte der Kunst des Alterthums (History of Ancient Art),* took part regularly in their professional discussions. That European art of the last third of the eighteenth, and much of the nineteenth centuries was dominated by Neoclassicism was largely the result of the theoretical and applied genius of these men.

Robert Adam remained faithful to the principles of this group. He worked with his friend Charles Louis Clérisseau (p. 240) in Rome, toured Italy with him, and also went with him to Spalato (Split). There, he prepared his "Ruins of the Palace of the Emperor Diocletian at Spalato in Dalmatia" (1764). In this design for an artificial ruin, Adam was too much of an artist to be content with merely reproducing archeological details. When he sketched the interior of a ruin, he was deeply concerned with achieving a three-dimensional effect. Piranesi, whom Adam knew personally, had the same ambition. Like Adam, the Italian master was trying to convey spatial effects in his works "Villa of Maecenas" and his "Frigidarium of Hadrian's Villa at Tivoli." Adam, Piranesi, and Hubert Robert (p. 146) were deeply impressed by the perfection of the "classical" forms which they saw in Roman ruins, but they were equally fascinated by the spatial organization of these ancient monuments.

Robert Adam

Drawing in India Ink of Architectural Compositions (One of Five).
Probably Executed in 1782. Soane Museum, London

It was characteristic of Adam that he was able to merge his experience as an archeological scholar with his creative abilities as an architect; and for this reason his creations are always fresher and more interesting than mere reconstructions. In a series of drawings called simply "Architectural Compositions," he gave his imagination free rein, choosing the ruinous state for his fictitious architecture. He obviously thought that allowing a flood of light to stream through the ruined vaults would aggrandize the proportions and make the whole composition more impressive.

Robert Wood

The Ruins of Balbec, Also Called Heliopolis. *London. 1757.*
Plate XXXV

Wood's two publications, *The Ruins of Balbec* and *The Ruins of Palmyra* (1753) enjoyed a tremendous popularity in England. Not only were they of interest to archeologists, but they also inspired those artists working in the second half of the eighteenth century who created "classical" artificial ruins as decorations for parks. Wood's renderings cannot compare in archeological reliability with those of Stuart and Revett (p. 216) whose designs became almost obligatory models for archeological representations of ruins. Nor does the abundance of widely dispersed fragments give a romantic effect, if we are to use the works of Stuart and Revett or Piranesi as a basis of comparison. For Piranesi, the total aesthetic impression was as important as scientific accuracy of observation.

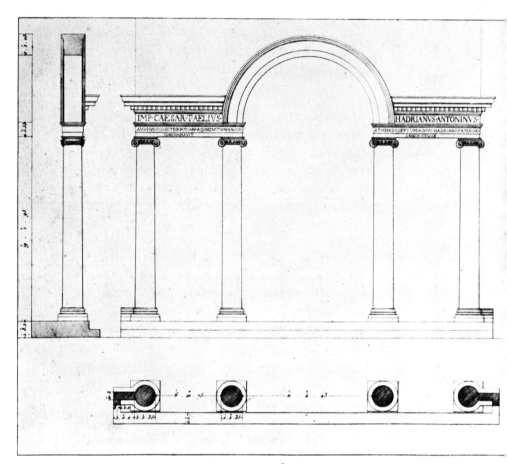

Stuart and Revett

Aqueduct of Hadrian in Athens. From Antiquities of Athens Measured and Delineated. *London. 1762-1830. Vol. III, Plate XXVI (1827). Elevation*

(PLEASE REFER TO PAGE 218)

216

Stuart and Revett

Aqueduct of Hadrian in Athens. From Antiquities of Athens Measured and Delineated. *London. 1762-1830. Vol. III, Plate XXVI.* *(1827)*

(PLEASE REFER TO PAGE 219)

Stuart and Revett

Next to Piranesi's publications, this series, issued by two English archeologists, was the most influential force in directing both scholars and amateur art-lovers toward a deeper, more intensive study of ancient ruins. Beethoven's "The Ruins of Athens," composed in 1812, echoes this renewed interest. The *Antiquities of Athens* contributed decisively to the gradual change from Rococo, with its colorful national variations, to an ever-increasing Classicism—more precisely, Neoclassicism. This trend had been anticipated by widespread interest in the excavations at Pompeii and Herculaneum (1748), and was further encouraged by Winckelmann's *History of the Art of Antiquity* and other archeological studies. In contrast to the heavily documented treatises of the Italian High Renaissance, which for the most part were read by scholars, the *Antiquities of Athens* offered both an accurate representation of famous buildings, and, more important, an aesthetic and historical approach which could easily be grasped by everyman.

Stuart and Revett

To understand the difference between Piranesi's etchings and the almost contemporary engravings of Stuart and Revett, we must keep in mind that Piranesi, regardless of his choice of subject, was primarily an artist, and then a student of archeology—though, to be sure, an ardent scholar in that field. Stuart and Revett were the reverse: scholars who looked first at the archeological aspects of the ruins, measuring them and representing them in their relationship to the surrounding landscape or town. The poetic and aesthetic potentialities of the scene were to them seemingly of secondary importance. The little genre pictures, of which there are many in Stuart and Revetts' oeuvre, do not betray an artistically high level, and are certainly not comparable with Piranesi's masterly prints. Even the proportions of the human figures to the monuments are faulty, as are the relationships between foreground figures and those further back. But even so, the *Antiquities of Athens,* with its numerous defects, has the virtue of conveying at least some idea of the fusion of past and present in eighteenth-century Greece.

Shugborough, Staffordshire

The West Front. Ca. 1769. With Stuart's Orangery and "Ruins."
Watercolor attributed to N. T. Dall. Ca. 1770.
(From English Country Houses *by Christopher Hussey)*

Thomas Anson, a member of the Society of Dilettanti founded in 1732 "for the encouragement of Greek taste and Roman spirit," commissioned James Stuart, architect and archeologist, to decorate his country seat of Shugborough.   Anson had already financed the publication of Stuart and Revetts' *Antiquities of Athens*.   Stuart erected a rather free variation of the Arch of Hadrian, and other "classical" ruins in the park of Anson's beautiful estate; placing them, paradoxically, next to some rococo structures.   It is intriguing to encounter such romanticized artificial ruins created by an artist better known for his very accurate delineations of classical buildings and monuments.   Stuart's activities as a practicing architect were not limited to Shugborough.   He built a Doric temple at Hagley which became nearly as famous an example of the Greek style of the 1770's as Strawberry Hill of the Gothic, and a neo-classical town house—also for the Anson family—in London's St. James's Square.

James Stuart was a representative of an "in-between" generation, and was not, as many have said, the last of the Palladians.   On the one hand he indulged, archeologically and architecturally, in classical reminiscences.   Yet at the same time he was still tied to the rococo heritage, and vacillated between the erudite scholarship of the archeologist and the playfulness of that style.

Desert De Retz

*Drawing for a Column-Shaped Residence. Built in 1771. From Os-
vald Sirén.* China and Gardens of Europe of the Eighteenth Century.
Plate LXXXV

The park of Monsieur de Monville was decorated with playful-looking little buildings which varied in style from a Greek Temple of Pan, to a vine-covered pyramid, to a house in the "Chinese manner." This residence, in the form of a partially broken column whose top is decaying, represents yet another variant. The contrast between its function as a four-storey living quarter, and its very anti-functional shape is quite amusing. Even with the broadest toleration for the eccentricities of eighteenth-century architecture, this strange dichotomy between form and function is almost incomprehensible to us. It is still debated as to whether Hubert Robert (p. 146) inspired, or actually helped to design this odd building. In any case it is difficult to imagine that an artist so imbued with the spirit of antiquity could have consented to lend his help in creating a perversion of the Greek motif. It must be said, however, that this alienation from the original form and meaning of a classical column is no more grotesque than the use of a Roman altar motif in the design of Empire furniture.

Sir William Chambers

*Gardens and Buildings. Artificial Ruin of a Roman Arch. Designed
for the Roman Arch in Kew. 1759-60*

Although he had studied with Clérisseau, and exercised wide influence through his treatise *Civil Architecture* (1759), Sir William Chambers was not a great architect. Important because of his activities as a landscape architect, he was the most famous of the second generation of English landscapists who overcame, by means of their "natural" creations, the French formal "artificial" garden. He decorated his best-known work, the Gardens of Kew, with, among other things, the artificial ruins of a Roman arch, a pagoda, a mosque, and a pseudo-Gothic "cathedral." Chambers, who spent his youth in China, is best known for placing pleasant imitation-Chinese structures in parks and gardens. But he was more than just an advocate for the "jardin Anglo-Chinois," for he, even more than his predecessor William Kent, propagated the craze for studding landscaped parks with small buildings of every style.

He was stimulated by the enthusiasm of poets and writers like Thomas Gray and Horace Walpole, who admired these parks and their architectural embellishments, and who pleaded again and again for "Chinese-Gothic irregularity." Chambers, who had seen Rome, and who had fought against the regular geometric design of the French park, tried to incorporate in his works ideas similar to those of Kent, "the father of modern gardening."

The artificial ruin represented the pièce de résistance in the vocabulary of architectural decoration of parks and gardens. Chambers was still subconsciously reflecting Palladian rules—the "decay" of this Roman arch is rather orderly and symmetrical. Later, Roman ruins in English parks would become more irregular—more intimately fused with the processes of natural growth—and therefore more romantic.

Schönbrunn, near Vienna, Austria

Built by J. F. Hohenberg. 1777. Photo, Austrian Tourist Office, New York

ARTIFICIAL RUINS

When Maria Theresa of Austria commissioned the construction of the Castle of Schönbrunn, she wanted a building which would surpass in grandeur Louis XIV's Versailles. Schönbrunn, which eventually became her favorite residence, was planned, and for the most part completed, by the great Johann Fischer von Erlach, whose personal style shows both Roman baroque and classical traits. As in the parks surrounding Versailles and other eighteenth-century seats of royalty, there were numerous other smaller buildings. At Schönbrunn, the "Gloriette," set on top of the hill where the palace had originally been planned, became the focal point of the park. The court architect, Johann Ferdinand von Hohenberg, who designed the "Gloriette" and the park, also erected an obelisk and an artificial ruin—the latter a Roman arch which he named "The Ruins of Carthage." Hohenberg was a professor at the Academy of Architecture in Vienna, and had studied in Rome, where he became the first German member of the French Academy there. As a typical intellectual classicist, he was influenced by Winckelmann's work, and Piranesi's interest in the aesthetic potentialities of decayed architecture. So it is not surprising, that in spite of the architect's desire to create something genuinely classical-looking, that upon its completion the arch turned out to be rather poetic and romantic. With the beautifully landscaped park as setting, overlooking a reed-filled pond, enlivened by marble nymphs, its outlines softened by foliage, it became the "elegy in stone" before which Mozart and Beethoven loved to dream.

Carlo Marchionni

Villa Albani, Rome. Tempietto Diruto. Ca. 1760. Fototeca di Architettura e Topografia dell'Italia Antica

Carlo Marchionni was the court architect of Cardinal Albani, for whose collections Johann Joachim Winckelmann became the curator. Winckelmann's influence on Albani and on his architect shows clearly in the employ of Greek form and in the complete neglect of Roman tradition.

This extremely elegant, too well-groomed looking ruin exemplifies the basic difference between the Italian and the English approach to this kind of architecture. If one compares, for instance, the classical artificial ruin of the Temple of Bacchus at Paineshill, Surrey (p. 204), or Virginia Water in Windsor Great Park (p. 206) with the Tempietto, the contrast becomes obvious. For the Italian structure is merely ornamental—a combination of classical and Hellenistic forms with some Palladian reminiscenses—not really Greek and not really neo-classical. Even the original fragments of ancient buildings which are incorporated into it do not relieve this impression of eclecticism. It is typical of the transitional period which preceded true Neoclassicism in Italy. The psychological, as well as the formal approaches of the two schools of architecture were entirely different: the English wanted the beholder to respond emotionally to the associations evoked by decay; to reflect about what he was looking at, whereas the Italians, ignoring deeper symbolic connotations, wanted to create a showpiece; a decoration which would be unsurpassed in beauty; another jewel to grace the collection of a prelate.

Imitation of the Front of the Temple of Antonino and Faustina

Villa Borghese, Rome. Nineteenth Century. Fototeca di Architettura e Topografia dell'Italia Antica

The eighteenth-century architect or amateur builder of artificial ruins frequently combined elements of original structures with his more or less arbitrary inventions. The desire to be archeologically reliable, or merely decorative, or to express nostalgic feelings for a vanished past often dictated the aesthetic function of these fragments. The noble columns of Virginia Water (p. 206) are an example of this kind of eclectic architecture done in good taste. However, the acute emotional receptivity of the eighteenth century to the past was to become the blatant historicism of the nineteenth century, which preferred to see imitations of Greek, Roman, or medieval structures.

This theatrical prop, erected in the park of the Villa Borghese, in no way represents what we have called artificial ruins, in spite of the careful, conscious effort to make it appear antique. It is a cheap-looking showpiece of watered-down Neoclassicism, without any artistic merit whatsoever, an apotheosis of the commonplace. Worse yet, it was built in a city which contained an abundance of ancient remains.

The original temple, erected by Antoninus Pius in 141 A.D., which stood at the north side of the Forum, was incorporated in 1602 into the baroque church of San Lorenzo in Miranda, and is extant. The ugly discrepancy between the still aesthetically meaningful remainders of the original ancient temple, and the specious, hollow quality of the overly correct textbook architecture shows clearly that the era of the artificial ruin has ended.

Artificial Roman Ruin

From Grohmann, Ideenmagazin. *1797*

(PLEASE REFER TO PAGE 234)

G. B. Piranesi

Aqueduct of Nero. From Views of Rome, *Plate LV. 1775. The Metropolitan Museum of Art, Rogers Fund, 1941*

(PLEASE REFER TO PAGE 235)

Artificial Roman Ruin

The juxtaposition of an artificial ruin and a genuine Roman aqueduct as it looked in the eighteenth century shows how important it was that the creator of a sham structure have a sense of empathy with the classical past, as well as with organic nature. Gifted eighteenth-century artists such as William Chambers and Robert Adam (pp. 224, 208), possessed these qualities, and as a result their artificial ruins achieved a harmonious balance between artifice and environment. Here, highly intellectualized literary Romanticism has dictated the style; one feels the uncomfortable presence of a "motif." There is no sense of the graceful architectural rhythms inherent in the arches of the ruined aqueduct; rhythms which Piranesi captured so well in his engravings.

G. B. Piranesi

There is a tremendous dignity in this array of simple, functional arches; man-made forms which the invasion of Nature has rendered even more beautiful. In contrast to Grohmann's boring, repetitious imitation of a ruin, Piranesi's etching conveys the charm of both the stone surface and the organic growth which clings to it. The result is an enchanting interplay between the monumentality of the aqueduct and its living ornamentation.

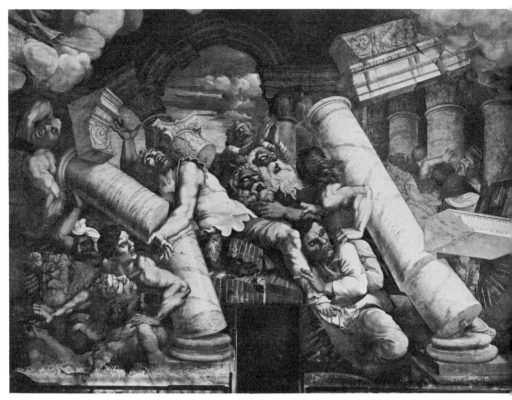

Giulio Romano

*Collapse of the Giants' Hall. Fresco from the Palazzo del Tè,
Mantua. 1534. Alinari Art Reference Bureau*

For many years, Giulio Romano worked under Raphael in Rome, helping the master to create such works as the frescoes telling the story of Amor and Psyche (Villa Farnesina), the murals in the Sala del Incendio (Vatican), and his last work, the "Transfiguration." Later, the Duke of Mantua commissioned Romano to design and decorate the Palazzo del Tè.

In this grandiose, somewhat brutal fresco, Raphael's pupil introduced a new motif which would be widely imitated. This was the ruin, conceived not as *fait accompli*—the results of the gradual exposure of architecture to the forces of natural and human destructiveness—but at that precise catastrophic instant—that "transitory moment" when the intact building became a ruin. Following Ovid's myth of the War Between the Gods and the Giants, Romano depicted the defeat of the latter, and the collapse of a monumental temple. His sensationalistic description of the disaster—bursting walls, cracking arches and vaults, falling columns, and the horrified expressions of the stricken giants—displeased both contemporary artists and future critics. Jacob Burckhardt complained about the absence here of that serene balance so typical of High-Renaissance art; a balance for which Raphael was particularly noted. For even when Romano's master depicted such terrible events as the "Conflagration of the Borgo" (Vatican), he retained his sense of poise and rhythmical order.

Using Mantegna's devices to achieve perspective, as well as Correggio's wide-angled panoramic composition, Giulio Romano developed a kind of pre-baroque illusionism which stimulated seventeenth and eighteenth-century artists as much as it offended his contemporaries.

237

Pommersfelden Castle, Bavaria

Ruin Room. Frescoes by Marchini. 1716-18

The sham quality of all of these artificial ruins becomes even more evident if they are not three-dimensional works; for an artificial ruin which has the dimension of depth is always more suggestive, even if made from flimsy material. Here, an ordinary room has been changed into the interior of a ruin by the clever use of illusionistic ceiling and wall frescoes. Remembrances of Giulio Romano's frescoes in the Palazzo del Tè in Mantua, or Gregorio de Ferrari's Sala delle Rovine in the Genoese Palazzo Balbi-Grappello may have given Giovanni Francesco Marchini the idea of making a room in Pommersfelden Castle appear as a ruin. This Italian artist was commissioned as court painter to Lothar Franz von Schönborn, and was ordered to create something comparable to the great Italian illusionistic works. It is easy to see that he was influenced by the fantastic virtuosity of Andrea Pozzo in shaping the illusion of spatial extension. Surrounded in this relatively small room by Marchini's tumbling architectural debris, the spectator thinks he is actually witnessing this faked catastrophe.

As is typical in Italian decorative style around 1700, the ceiling seems to open up, and angels, floating in space, calmly observe the shifting, disintegrating scene below. Cupola and drum crack; vaults burst; balustrades and supporting pillars crumble. Naked men strive unsuccessfully to halt the process of destruction—straining to support the toppling architecture with their bodies. The fleeting moment is captured in the best baroque tradition, and the immediacy of the catastrophe is emphasized by extremely realistic details. The baroque love of the sensational and of extraordinary events is combined with the romantic preoccupation with arousing reflections about the transiency of human life and creations.

In a similar, but less dramatic vein, Marchini later decorated the oval vestibule of the Electoral Palace built by Johann Balthasar Neumann for Hugo Damian Schönborn. Here, the theme of impermanence is less evident, and rustic masonry suggested by Italian grottoes is used as decorative motif.

Charles Louis Clérisseau

Detail of a Design for a Ruin Room at Trinità dei Monti, Rome. Designed and Executed in 1766. Courtesy, Prof. Thos. J. McCormick

(PLEASE REFER TO PAGE 242)

Charles Louis Clérisseau

Design for a Ruin Room at Trinità dei Monti, Rome. Designed and Executed in 1766. Courtesy, Prof. Thos. J. McCormick

(PLEASE REFER TO PAGE 243)

241

Charles Louis Clérisseau

It is interesting to compare Clérisseau's designs with the ruins painted by Marchini in the Garden Room of Pommersfelden (p. 238). The Frenchman's classicist approach was static, whereas the Italian artist, fifty years earlier, had dynamically pictured the structures at the moment of their collapse; dramatizing, in typical baroque fashion, the crumbling of the walls and vaults and the annihilation of the human figures. This change from the depiction of the most dramatic moment of the catastrophe to the illustration of the relatively static results of the successive stages of decay is more characteristic of the transition from baroque to classical modes than any modification in individual architectural forms.

Charles Louis Clérisseau

Clérisseau was a close friend and co-worker of the Adam brothers, and Robert Adam especially was an outspoken admirer of his works. Later, the French artist assisted Thomas Jefferson in the design of the Virginia State House. Clérisseau belonged to the same circle of the neo-classicist avant-garde, centered in Rome, as the archeologist Johann Winckelmann and the painter Raphael Mengs. He accompanied Robert Adam to Spalato (Split) in 1754. As a pupil of J. F. Blondel (p. 142), and later, in Rome, of Giovanni Paolo Pannini (p. 122), Clérisseau applied the newly developed concepts in his own special manner by deploying ruins as illusionistic decorations of interiors. His aim was twofold: to decorate the room as a continuous spatial unit, and to create the illusion of three-dimensional reality; of an artificial ruin. Clérisseau may have been stimulated by ancient Roman and Pompeian interiors in which the decorator had tried to imitate architecture.

Waghäusel (near Bruchsal)

Part of Painted Ceiling. After 1730. Hirmer Photoarchiv, Munich

Cardinal Damian von Schönborn played a leading role among the many princes of the Church, who by their generous commissions aided and influenced the development of German baroque architecture and decoration. Even among the members of the remarkable Schönborn family, many of whom were cardinals, archbishops, and patrons of the arts, Damian distinguished himself for his passionate devotion to the construction of castles, monasteries, and residences. These he surrounded with magnificent parks which were enhanced with fashionable architectural "follies." Waghäusel is one of these "follies." It is a small retreat, constructed in a strictly symmetrical design. The central room, conceived as a hermitage for meditation, is in keeping with the contemporary fad for this manner of decoration. In 1730 the Cardinal wrote from Rome to his architect Johann Michael Ludwig Rohrer ordering him to decorate the room with stucco and painting "auf eremitisch"—as a hut for a hermit. The perforated, dilapidated-looking roof rests on pieces of Roman ruins, and other fragments appear in the background. Vegetation has worked its way into the roof and intensifies the effect of decay. Intimate details—almost still lifes—show a typically German predilection for "Gemütlichkeit" (see also Altdorfer, p. 36). Paradoxically, these agreeable details exist in a setting from which on principle even the smallest pleasures of the world should be ruthlessly excluded. Rohrer's rather comfortable hermit's cell, with its charming decorations by Marchini, betrays the attempt to stir up the same emotions, genuine or assumed, as those evoked by the "follies" found in English and French parks.

THE
TWENTIETH
CENTURY

Twentieth Century

One should be extremely cautious in the analysis of contemporary art. Comprehensive books on the general history of art, excellent as they may be in their presentation of the works of the past, are often marred by their evaluations of the art created by the author's own generation. Judgments concerning the creations of the preceding generation often seem to be dictated by contemporary slogans and fads instead of critical insight. Artists who have been highly praised in ebullient adjectives are often completely forgotten after twenty years, or, equally cruelly, are considered amusing failures. Thus, the following four contemporary works are included here only with reluctance—as evidence of the reaction of modern man to ruins, a motif which appears relatively seldom in paintings of our time.

The post-Romanticism and pseudo-Romanticism which characterized so much of nineteenth-century literature and art produced indirectly the absurdities of middle-class *kitsch*, a futile attempt to alleviate the ugly realities of urbanization and industrialism. Genuine deep feeling for nature became diluted, and degenerated into cozy sweetness or pseudo-exoticism. A silvery moon, preferably framed in dramatic clouds, a melancholy, innocent maiden, caves, craggy rocks, a dreamy lake, and—last not least—a ruin, became indispensable. Those same ingredients, which were often genuinely moving in eighteenth-century paintings, soon lost all of their suggestive power.

Nevertheless, the contemporary intellectual, basing his judgment only on nineteenth-century run-of-the-mill productions, and calling any sort of interest in ruins old-fashioned and philistine, is being grossly unfair. He damns the entire motif, lumping an etching of a ruin by Piranesi together with obviously sentimentalized representations of the same theme in paintings, illustrations, and even postcards. This is like comparing a family scene by Norman Rockwell with one by the seventeenth-century Dutch painter Pieter de Hooch. This contempt for ruins was equally characteristic of the "avant garde" of twenty or thirty years ago, which was disgusted by tourist traps such as Carcassonne and Rothenburg—euphemistically called "architectural restorations."

It is possible that now, in the second half of the twentieth century, the ruin may again become meaningful in art. Two major wars and many revolutions, recorded on photographs and in movies, have brought countless images of demolished buildings before our eyes, though in our haste to destroy and rebuild we have lost the awareness of the patient, deliberate, and often beautiful wearing away of stone by time—the fascination of decay.

Peter Blume

*The Eternal City. 1937. Collection. The Museum of Modern Art,
New York. Mrs. Simon Guggenheim Fund*

The ruins of the Roman Forum have been depicted again and again, either as more or less accurate representations, or as elements of a meaningful townscape. This modern painter conceives the act of destruction as the result not of natural catastrophe or enemy soldiers, but as a crime committed by the forces of evil personified by Mussolini as Jack-in-the-box. The mere glance of "Il Duce" is sufficient to smash ancient sculpture and architecture. People are being tortured and killed in the background; others crouch in the oppressive chambers of subterranean vaults. The sadism of the dictator leaves no place to hide. A martyred, Christ-like figure is enshrined in the interior of a ruined house. In this painting the ruin is equivalent to chaos. Not a trace of classical greatness remains, and the scene in no way suggests the center of the city which once ruled and helped to civilize the Western World.

O. L. Guglielmi

Mental Geography. Courtesy the Downtown Gallery, New York.
Collection of Mrs. Edith Gregor Halpert

In Heemskerck's "Jericho" (p. 26) there are smashed stones and crumbling mortar. Here are twisted steel cables and strangely warped iron girders. But both works convey similar meanings. The ruins of Jericho are symbolic of universal destruction and death, while Guglielmi's surrealistic painting of the Brooklyn Bridge represents the dissolution of what man likes to consider indestructible: these are images of far more than local disasters; they represent the end of civilization as humans define it: annihilation without hope of resurrection.

John Piper

A Ruined House. 1941. Marlborough Fine Art Ltd., London

There is a quality of frightening shrillness in the light which strikes the walls of this melancholy house and renders it the color of chalk. The ruin dominates the landscape, the village in the background, and even the sky, and makes the painting as nihilistic and pessimistic as Guglielmi's. As we enter this landscape, we lose all confidence in Nature; the mind dissolves in the empty space and turbid patches of color.

Ben Shahn

Liberation. Collection of James Thrall Soby, The Museum of Modern Art, New York

Different as they may be, the three examples of twentieth-century art shown here express the climax of despair and complete hopelessness. Shahn's painting, in contrast, being equally bitter and cynical, and without illusions, still says "yes" to the possibility of resurrection—of which "liberation" represents one small step. There are children at play; poor creatures terrified by their wartime experiences, floating around a giant-stride before the unbelievably sad open entrails of the smashed house—but yet, they seem to float above all this misery.

"How much more of this is there before we come to something?"

SELECTED BIBLIOGRAPHY

Selected Bibliography

The titles listed refer exclusively to books and illustrated folios which are pertinent to the topic of ruins. Monographs on individual artists or particular places are included only insofar as they contribute to our specific problem.

Adam, Robert. *Ruins of the Palace of the Emperor Diocletian at Spalato in Dalmatia.* London, 1764.

Baldass, Ludwig von. *Hieronymus Bosch.* Vienna, 1943.

Beers, Henry Augustin. *A History of English Romanticism in the 18th Century.* New York, 1932.

Bibiena, Ferdinando Galli. *Varie Opere di Prospettiva.* Bologna, 1703-1708.

Blondel, Jacques François. *Livre Nouveau ou Règles des Cinq Ordres d'Architecture* par Jacques Barozzio de Vignole. Paris, 1767.

Boetzkes, Ottilie G. *Salvator Rosa, Seventeenth-Century Italian Painter, Poet and Patriot.* New York, 1960.

Casella, M. T. *Francesco Colonna, biografia e opere.* Padua, 1959.

Caylus, Anne Claude Philippe, Comte de. *Recueil d'Antiquites.* Paris, 1752-1767.

Chambers, Sir William. *A Treatise on Civil Architecture.* London, 1759.

———, *Les Jardins Anglo-Chinois.* London, 1743.

Clark, Sir Kenneth. *The Gothic Revival.* New York, 1929.

———, *Landscape into Art.* London, 1949.

Collins, Thomas. *Designs for Pleasure and Recreation.* London, 1766.

Colonna, Francesco. *Hypnerotomachia Polifili.* Venice, 1499.

Constable, W. G. *Canaletto.* Oxford, 1962.

Cram, Ralph Adams. *The Ruined Abbeys of Great Britain.* Boston, 1927.

Crossley, Frederick Herbert. *The English Abbey.* London, 1942.

Cuitt, George, the Younger. *Wanderings and Pencillings Amongst Ruins of the Olden Time.* London, 1848.

De Tolnay, Charles. *Pierre Breughel l'Ancien.* Brussels, 1935.

Dickins, Lilian, and Stanton, Mary. *An 18th-century Correspondence: being the Letters of Dean Swift—Pitt—the Lytteltons and the Grenvilles—Lord Dacre . . . and others to Sanderson Miller, Esq. of Radway.* London, 1910.

Du Pérac. *I Vestigi dell'Antichità di Roma.* (Paris), 1575.

Dyer, John. *The Ruins of Rome.* 1720.

Geiger, Benno. *Magnasco.* Bergamo, 1949.

261

Gibbon, Edward. *The History of The Decline and Fall of the Roman Empire*. London, 1776.

Gilpin, William. *Observations on the River Wye and several parts of South Wales, relative chiefly to picturesque beauty.* . . . London, 1782.

———— *Three Essays: on Picturesque Beauty; on Picturesque Travel.* . . . London, 1792.

Glueck, Gustav. *Peter Brueghel the Elder*. New York, 1956.

Goering, Max. *Francesco Guardi*. Vienna, 1944.

Gothein, Marie Luise. *A History of Garden Art*. London, 1928.

Gray, Thomas. *Correspondence of Thomas Gray, Walpole, West and Ashton.* . . . Oxford, 1915.

Grohmann, Johann Gottfried (edit.). *Ideenmagazin für Liebhaber von Gärten, englischen Anlagen.* . . . Leipzig, 1797.

Hartt, Frederick. *Giulio Romano*. New Haven, 1958.

Heemskerck, Marten van. *Die römischen Skizzenbücher im Königlichen Kupferstich-Kabinett, Berlin.* 1913.

Hirschfeld, Christian C. L. *Theorie der Garten Kunst*. Leipzig, 1777-1782.

Home, Henry, see Kames, Henry Home.

Hussey, Christopher. *The Picturesque*. London-New York, 1927.

James, Henry. *Abbeys and Castles*. 1877.

James, M. R., and Thompson, A. H. *Abbeys*. London, 1926.

Jones, Barbara M. *Follies and Grottoes*. London, 1953.

Kames, Henry Home. *Elements of Criticism*. Edinburgh, 1762.

Langley, Batty. *New Principles of Gardening*. London, 1728.

Le Rouge, Georges Louis. *Jardins Anglo-Chinois*. 1785.

Macaulay, Rose. *Pleasure of Ruins*. London, 1953.

Mac Swiny, Eugene. *Tombeaux Des Princes Des Grands Capitaines.* . . . Paris, 1737-38.

Manwaring, Elizabeth Wheeler. *Italian Landscape in 18th-Century England*. New York, 1925.

Mayor, A. Hyatt. *The Bibiena Family*. New York, 1945.

———— *Giovanni Battista Piranesi*. New York, 1952.

McCormick, Thomas J. *"A Ruin Room by Clérisseau," The Connoisseur*, Vol. CXLIX, No. 602, 1962.

Moeller, L. *Der Wrangelschrank und die verwandten süddeutschen Intarsienmoebel des 16. Jahrhunderts.* Berlin, 1956.

Palladio, Andrea. *Le Antichità di Roma*. Venice, 1554.

Piper, John. *"Pleasing Decay," Architectural Review*, Sept. 1947.

Piranesi, Giovanni Battista. *Le Antichità Romane*. Rome, 1756.

————*Della Magnificenza ed Architettura de' Romani*. Rome, 1761-1762.

————*Varie Vedute di Roma*. Rome, 1748.

Pozzo, Andrea. *Rules and Examples of Perspective proper for Painters and Architects*. Transl. by J. James. London, 1707.

Price, Sir Uvedale. *An Essay on the Picturesque as Compared with the Sublime and the Beautiful.* . . London, 1794.

Pueckler-Muskau, Hermann Ludwig Heinrich. *Andeutungen über Landschaftsgärtnerei.* . . Stuttgart, 1834.

Ritchie, Andrew C. *English Painters. Hogarth to Constable*. Baltimore, 1942.

Sadeler, Egidius (Gilles). *Vestigi della Antichità di Roma, Tivoli, Pozzvolo et Altri Lvochi. . .* Prague, 1616.

Sanderson-Miller. *See* Dickens, L. and Stanton, M.

Scamozzi, Vincenzo. *Discorsi sopra l'Antichità di Roma.* Venice, 1582.

Scharf, Alfred. *The Fantastic Visions of Monsù Desiderio.* Exhibition, John and Marble Ringling Museum of Art, Sarasota, Fla., 1950.

Scherer, Margaret R. *Marvels of Ancient Rome.* New York, 1955.

Schmoll, J. A. Eisenwerth (edit.). *Das Unvollendete als künstlerische Form. Ein Symposium.* Saarbrücken. Berne and Munich 1959.

Scholz, János (edit.), introd. by A. H. Mayor. *Baroque and Romantic Stage Design.* New York, 1950.

Serlio, Sebastiano. *Il Libro terzo. . . Antichità di Roma.* Venice, 1540.

Simmel, George. *Die Ruine. Zur Philosophie der Kunst.* Potsdam, 1922.

Sirén, Osvald. *China and Gardens of Europe of the Eighteenth Century.* New York, 1950.

Stuart, James, and Revett, Nicholas. *The Antiquities of Athens.* London, 1762-1830.

Summerson, John H. *Heavenly Mansions.* New York, 1963.

Swinburne, Henry. *Travels in the Two Sicilies.* Dublin, 1783.

Vasi, Giuseppe Agostino. *Delle Magnificenze di Roma.* Rome, 1747-1761.

Vignola, Giacomo Barozzio. *Regola delli Cinque Ordini d'Architettura.* 1562.

Vitruvius, Pollio Marcus. *I Dieci Libri dell' Architettura.* Venice, 1567.

Vogel, Hans. *Die Ruine in der Darstellung der Abendländischen Kunst.* Kassel, 1948.

Volney, Constantin François Chasseboeuf, Comte de. *Ruins, or Meditations on the Revolution of Empires.* 1791.

Von Einem, Herbert. *Caspar David Friedrich.* Berlin, 1938.

Wackenroder, Wilhelm Heinrich. *Herzensergiessungen eines kunstliebenden Klosterbruders.* Berlin, 1797.

Walpole, Horace. *Letters.* edit. by Paget Toynbee. 1903-1905.

Warton, Thomas. *Pleasures of Melancholy.* 1745.

Whately, Thomas. *Observations on Modern Gardening.* London, 1770.

Winckelmann, Johann Joachim. *Geschichte der Kunst des Alterthums.* Dresden, 1764.

Wittkower, Rudolf. *Architectural Principles in the Age of Humanism.* New York, 1965.

Wood, Robert. *Ruins of Balbec.* London, 1757.

————— *Ruins of Palmyra.* London, 1753.

Wright, William. *Grotesque Architecture, or Rural Amusement.* London, 1767.

Zampetti, Pietro. *I Vedutisti Veneziani del Settecento. Catalogo della Mostra.* Venice, 1967.

INDEX

Index

269

Poussin, Nicolas (1594-1665) 47, 50, 53, 55, 65, 109, 119, 137, 162, 196
Pozzo, Andrea (1642-1709) 239

Raphael (Raffaello Sanzio) (1483-1520) 127, 154, 237
Rembrandt Harmensz van Rijn (1606-1669) 49, 69
Retz, Desert de. See Desert de Retz
Revett, Nicholas (ca. 1720-1804) 120, 215-21
Ricci, Marco (1676-1729) 70, 147
Ricci, Sebastiano (1659-1734) 48, 70, 147
Richard de Burgh, Earl of Ulster. See Ulster
Richard the Lion-Hearted, King (1157-1199) 177
Rinuccini, Ottavio (1562-1621) 102
Rip van Winkle 183
Robert, Hubert (1733-1808) 48, 120, 146, 148, 150, 152, 153, 157, 211, 223
Rockwell, Norman (1894-   ) 248
Rohrer, Johann Michael Ludwig (1683-1732) 245
Romano, Giulio 236, 239
Rome, Aqueduct of Nero 233
  Arch of Janus Quadrifons 146
  Arch of Septimius Severus 22
  Argentina Theater 113
  Basilica of St. Maxentius 80
  Colosseum 53, 64, 110, 113, 119, 122
  Column of Trajan 119, 122, 123
  Concordia Temple 22
  Forum of Nerva 24, 130
  Hadrian's Villa 130
  Marcus Aurelius, statue of 122, 123
Rome, Nymphaeum Aquae Julia 30, 183
  Pantheon 122, 123
  Piazza Vittorio Emanuele II 31
  Pyramid of Cestius 119, 122
  Roman Forum 22, 33, 52, 54, 62, 128, 231, 250
  Temple of Castor 123, 128
  Temple of Jupiter Stator 22
  Temple of Jupiter Tonans 22
  Thermae of Caracalla 28
  Trinità dei Monti 240, 241
  Vatican 237
  Villa Albani 228
  Villa Borghese 230
  Villa Farnesina 237
Rosa, Salvator (1615-1673) 47, 48,
51, 56, 137, 162, 196
Rothenburg, Germany 248
Rousseau, Jean-Jacques (1712-1778) 161, 198
Ruisdael, Jacob van (1628-1682) 49, 67, 68, 162, 181, 185
Runge, Philipp Otto (1777-1810) 185

Sadeler, Egidius (1570-1629) 13, 30, 183
St. James's Palace 129
Salvadori, Andrea (act. 1625) 104
Sanderson-Miller 196
Sanmartino, Giuseppe (1720-1793) 99
Sbarra, F. (Second half 17th Century) 107
Scamozzi, Vincenzo (1552-1616) 11, 22, 131
Schinkel, Karl Friedrich (1781-1841) 115
Schönborn, Cardinal Damian von 239, 245
Schönborn, Lothar Franz von (1655-1729) 239
Schönbrunn Castle 197, 226
Schwind, Moritz von (1804-1871) 185
Scott, Walter (1771-1832) 199
Serlio, Sebastiano (1475-1554) 11, 16, 19, 145
Sforza Book of Hours 34, 37
Shahn, Ben (1898-   ) 256
Shovell, Sir Clowdisley (1650-1707) 70, 72, 147
Sibylla, Temple of. See Tivoli
Soane, Sir John (1753-1837) 157
Society of Dilettanti 162, 221
Sodom 11, 27
Sotalbo, Spain 4
Spalato (Split), Yugoslavia 211, 243
Spera, Clemente (ca. 1700) 78
Spitzweg, Carl (1808-1885) 185
Stowe 196
Strawberry Hill 57, 162, 221
Stuart, James (1713-1788) 120, 215-21

Tardieu, Nicolas (1716-1791) 72
Teatro Olimpico 102, 107
Telari 102
Tiepolo, Giovanni Battista (1696-1770) 76, 83, 86
Tintern Abbey 164, 166, 167, 191
Tischbein, Johann H. W. (1751-1829) 126

270

Tivoli, Temple of Sibylla 124, 134, 135, 138, 139, 162
Toile de Jouy. See Jouy
Torelli, Giacomo (1604-1678) 107
Travi, Antonio (1608-1665) 60
Troy 11
Turner, Joseph Mallord William (1775-1851) 167

Ulster, Earl of 175
Urbino, Duke of 195
Uxmal, Yucatán 3

Valdés Leal, Juan de (1622-1690) 69
Vasari, Giorgio (1511-1574) 195
Versailles, Park of 149, 163, 227
Vesalius, Andreas (1514-1564) 11
Vignola, Giacomo Barozzi da (1507-1573) 11, 142, 144
Vinci, Leonardo da (1452-1519) 11
Virginia Water 196, 206, 229, 231
Vitruvius, Pollio Marcus (1st century B.C.) 11, 18
Vivaldi, Antonio (1675-1741) 3

Volney, Constantin François Chasseboeuf (1757-1820) 198
Volpini, Joseph (died 1729) 203
Voltaire, François-Marie Arouet (1694-1778) 120

Wackenroder, Wilhelm Heinrich (1773-1798) 197
Waghäusel 244
Wallpaper 141
Walpole, Horace (1717-1797) 57, 81, 129, 161, 162, 196, 199, 205, 225
Warton, Thomas (1728-1790) 162
Weimar, Germany 197
Weyden, Rogier van der (1400-1464) 37
Winckelmann, Johann Joachim (1717-1768) 120, 127, 132, 211, 218, 227, 229, 243
Wood, Robert (1717?-1771?) 121, 214
Wörlitz, Germany 197
Wrangelschrank 20
Wright of Derby, Joseph (1734-1797) 178